WHERE THE SHADOWS LIE

WHERE THE SHADOWS LIE

A JUNGIAN INTERPRETATION OF TOLKIEN'S *THE LORD OF THE RINGS*

PIA SKOGEMANN

Chiron Publications
Wilmette, Illinois

Originally published as *En Jungiansk Fortolkning af Tolkiens Ringenes Herre*. ©
2004 by Pia Skogemann. Published by Forlaget Athene.

Book and cover design by Marianne Jankowski

Cover art by Pia Skogemann

Printed in the United States of America

Library of Congress Cataloging-in-Publication Data
Skogemann, Pia.
    [En Jungiansk Fortolkning af Tolkiens Ringenes Herre. English]
    Where the shadows lie : a Jungian interpretation of Tolkien's The lord
of the rings / Pia Skogemann.
        p. cm.
    "Originally published as En Jungiansk Fortolkning af Tolkiens Ringenes
Herre. c2004 by Pia Skogemann. Published by Forlaget Athene."
    Includes bibliographical references and index.
    ISBN 978-1-888602-45-6 (alk. paper)
    1. Tolkien, J. R. R. (John Ronald Reuel), 1892-1973. Lord of the rings.
    2. Archetype (Psychology) in literature. 3. Fantasy fiction, English--
History and criticism--Theory, etc. I. Title.

PR6039.O32L637166 2009
823'.912--dc22

                                                            2009012519

CONTENTS

Introduction   vii

1   Faëry or the Collective Unconscious   1

2   The Archetype of Consciousness: The Hobbits   9

3   The Journey Out: Archetypes of Transformation   55

4   The Trickster   77

5   The Hero   85

6   The Anima   103

7   The Love Story: Éowyn and Faramir   113

8   The Old King   123

9   The Spirit   129

10   The One Ring and the Three Elven Rings   145

11   The Collective Shadow   153

12   The End of an Age   167

13   Anthropos: The Cosmic Man   183

14   The Renewal of the Shire   193

Notes   201

Literature   203

Index   207

INTRODUCTION

I have written this book for readers who love *The Lord of the Rings* and for those who would like to read the trilogy, but don't know how to get started. My aim is to illustrate how C. G. Jung's theory of archetypes offers an important key to understanding the powerful imagery of Tolkien's masterpiece—and thereby a key to understanding ourselves.

I use Jungian theory as a tool for interpreting the story as the journey progresses through Middle-earth, but it is not a prerequisite to be acquainted with Jungian terminology in order to read this book. However, for readers who would like definitions and explanations, there is a good Jungian lexicon at http://www.nyaap.org.

This book is not a psycho-biographical analysis of Tolkien, and neither is it a tracing back to the origins of the figures and motives in Tolkien's universe. His knowledge of ancient myth, legends, and fairy tales was enormous, but he took all that material out of their old contexts and used them for a new purpose.

I understand *The Lord of the Rings* as a symbolic, not allegorical story. For example, instead of seeing World War II as an allegorical equivalent to *The Lord of the Rings*, the war, in my opinion, might be considered an example of how we are living in a world today in which the Ring has not yet been destroyed.

What interests me first and foremost is the impact of Tolkien's trilogy on readers' minds. We might perceive the contents of the trilogy as a description of the collective unconscious of this era. In the trilogy, we are not confronted with the troubles of a distant past; we are, indeed, presented with the issues of today. What Tolkien's trilogy offers to its readers are suggestions as to how some of these problems might be dealt with, and possibly solved.

Some readers never make it through the first seventy pages of Tolkien's *The Lord of the Rings*, no matter how hard they try. They simply fall asleep reading the long introduction, while other readers devour the pages and fall in love with the book forever. Personally, I belong to the latter group of readers. During the thirty-odd years that I have read, reread, and loved *The Lord of the Rings*, I have never succeeded in pinpointing any characteristic personality traits or common denominators that might help to define which readers could be expected to fall into which category.

I sense that the two general reactions—either falling asleep or becoming enthralled—divulge a fundamental truth about the very substance of Tolkien's trilogy: to an unusual extent, it activates the subconscious fantasies of its readers. In chat forums on the Web, young readers reveal that they love to read *The Lord of the Rings* late at night, because it inspires them to dream their way into the Tolkien universe. However, the second group of readers, who are bored to tears and end up falling asleep, are not able to connect consciously to the imagery in Tolkien's fantastic tale.

Archetypal symbols build a bridge to the collective unconscious; these archetypes are to be found in religion and mythology, in fairy tales, dreams, and fantasies. *The Lord of the Rings* contains all of these elements, which interact intensely with the psyches of its readers. I'll give you an example of how this interaction takes place in real life: one day, when he was thirteen years old, Peter sat in his room and heard his parents quarrelling. At that very moment, Peter saw an orc come looming toward him. It struck him in the chest with a spear; he fell toward the frame of his bedroom door, sinking down onto the floor. A few moments later, his mother found him lying there, bruised and dazed.

It's not difficult to interpret the orc as a personification of the negative emotions that thirteen-year-old Peter experienced while his parents were quarrelling, but which he was unconscious of at the time. Peter was—and is today—a perfectly normal and healthy young man.

At the time when his parent quarreled, he responded to the attack of the orc by literally fighting back: he decided to start taking courses in martial arts and became very proficient at his new sport. Generally, orcs symbolize negative and aggressive impulses. If they don't have specific enemies to combat, they immediately begin to quarrel, and quickly kill each other.

The Lord of the Rings is so full of archetypal figures that it would be relevant to speculate whether Tolkien had been acquainted with the theories of Jung. We don't know if he was, but Tolkien would not have been able to write such a wonderful story by constructing his work with the use of a Jungian "recipe." While writing the script to his film, *Star Wars*, director George Lucas did actually try to create a Jungian universe, but in his first attempts to do so, he failed miserably. He then simply wrote the story—and later, when analyzing the completed script, he discovered that his story now contained all the archetypal figures that he originally had wanted to be represented in his film.

A Jungian approach to *The Lord of the Rings* seems to be so obviously relevant that you would expect a Jungian to have published an analysis of it long ago. Yet I found only one title using a Jungian approach, *The Individuated Hobbit* (1979) by Timothy O'Neill. This author, however, seems to have no professional training in analytical psychology.

While it is obvious that *The Lord of the Rings* is a story that invites a Jungian interpretation, the story itself is anything but obvious or banal. Archetypal images are so packed with meaning that people never think of asking what they really do mean. When archetypes "appear in practical experience . . . they are images and at the same time emotions" (Jung 1961a, par. 589). The archetype is not just an intellectual concept; only if the image "is charged with numinosity, that is, with psychic energy, then it becomes dynamic and will produce consequences" (ibid.).

This is clearly the case with *The Lord of the Rings*; the reader is filled with joy and dimmed by tears again and again. Furthermore, the archetypes are related to the patterns of human behavior, so it is not surprising that one popular way of responding to the figures in *The Lord of the Rings* is by participating in role-playing games.

Once I got to work on my interpretation, suddenly nothing seemed quite so clear; the material in the trilogy is truly profound and there are many layers to work with. I have chosen to interpret the tale at two psychological levels, according to the Jungian structural model of the psyche: the Shire represents consciousness and is the uppermost layer of the psyche. The four hobbits represent the ego in all its different aspects and phases of life. As readers, we tend to identify ourselves with them, and while the story is unfolding, we experience the world from the four hobbits' point of view: we travel with them, see, experience, and take in the world as they do. The hobbits represent the type of people that we feel comfortable identifying with: they are good and sensible human beings. The Shire in which they lived was:

> a district of well-ordered business; and there in that pleasant corner of the world they plied their well-ordered business of living, and they heeded less and less the world outside where dark things moved, until they came to think that peace and plenty were the rule in Middle-earth and the right of all sensible folk. (1:14)

I clearly remember that the first time I read *The Lord of the Rings*, I felt that the Shire might easily be a description of Denmark, the country in which I live. It would seem logical that the human societies in Rohan and Gondor would feel more familiar to the reader, but this was not the case. Hobbiton seemed much more familiar and normal. The boundaries of the Shire constitute the borders of consciousness. This consciousness is totally ignorant of the world beyond. The Shire is a rather isolated and self-sufficient region; psychologically, the Shire represents a naïve state of consciousness, threatened by dangerously overwhelming impulses from the collective unconscious.

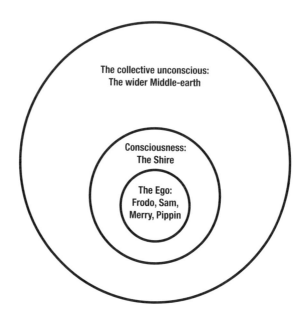

FIGURE I. *The Shire as a state of consciousness.*

Although the ego is extremely small and fragile at this stage compared to the vast kingdom of the unconscious, it is only through the reflecting and integrating activity of the ego-consciousness that a new psychological balance can be created in the individual. However, in order to achieve this goal, a dangerous quest awaits. For years, Frodo had been considering leaving the Shire to follow in Bilbo's footsteps, but he'd never gotten any further with his plans than daydreaming about it. Suddenly, Frodo no longer had a choice: he was being pursued by the Black Riders, who forced him to commence his quest. The inner necessity of undergoing an individuation process typically arises from a situation in life that is being experienced as extremely threatening.

The transition from the safe, familiar world to the beyond is marked by the meeting with Tom Bombadil in the Old Forest. Bombadil's kingdom is a frontier between consciousness and the unconscious. While Frodo and his friends are traveling from one destination to the next, they are often able to bring together what has been isolated and kept apart for ages. Foes become friends. Antagonists are reconciled, and not only do the hobbits make their mark on the world, the world certainly makes its mark upon them, too. Gradually, it becomes apparent that—like the Shire—almost all the different countries have become isolated; there is no communication between them. During the individuation process, the archetype of the Self is constellated, forming a stronger and clearer center, to which the ego then creates a new relationship. When Aragorn is crowned, he also reclaims the vast kingdom of his ancestors, in which the Shire is contained.

All four hobbits return home in a transformed state and are now able to carry out whatever is necessary in order to renew the Shire. In the end, a new set of boundaries have been created between the Shire and the rest of the world, prohibiting Big People from crossing into the Shire, while enabling all hobbits to travel freely and safely, wherever they would like to go.

On the journey, we meet many archetypal figures. Their historical backgrounds, dimensions, and meaningful correlations are either revealed or implied. Each of these characterizes archetypal aspects of the human psyche.

Clearly, the Ring is the strongest single symbol, and behind the golden ring lurks its maker. The Dark Lord, the

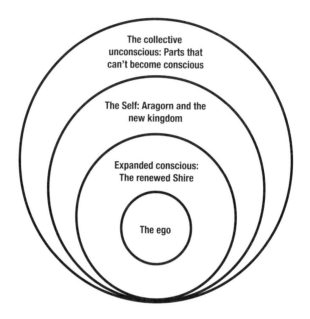

The collective
unconscious: Parts that
can't become conscious

The Self: Aragorn and the
new kingdom

Expanded conscious:
The renewed Shire

The ego

FIGURE 2. *The new kingdom as the Self*

Great Shadow, is the title character of the trilogy. Facing Sauron, the spirit of hatred, we have his strongest opponents, the bearers of the three rings: Elrond, Galadriel, and Gandalf. Galadriel is a magnificent *anima mundi* figure. She is a world soul. It is only fitting that her granddaughter, Arwen, is the anima partner of the young King Aragorn, whose father-in-law and stepfather Elrond represents the archetype of the Old King.

Gandalf is, of course, the Wise Old Man, the archetype of the spirit. He is the spirit who flies to and fro, the inspiring and enthusiastic initiator, who unites what the evil spirit seeks to disrupt. His shadow figure is the power-seeking Saruman, the negative spirit. Joined together, they could be compared to *Mercurius Duplex*, the patron spirit of the alchemists, at one and the same time good and evil.

Frodo is confronted with a much smaller shadow figure than Sauron and Saruman; he meets Gollum, who is more easily recognizable as the personal shadow of a human being. It would be tempting to identify the bearer of the ring as the main hero of the trilogy, but to do so would be to oversimplify the tale, for *The Lord of the Rings* contains so much more than a description of Frodo's individuation process. All the main characters undergo maturation processes and transformations. This offers the reader numerous possibilities of identifying with or mirroring a number of characters of both sexes and of varying ages. In addition to this, the reader can identify with many aspects of the characters. A friend of mine who is a political observer feels that much of his work resembles that of the eternally traveling Gandalf, while another friend who works as a healer mirrors herself in Gandalf in his capacity as a spiritual guide.

The Fellowship of the Ring is a central theme in the tale, but the true brotherhood does not consist of the group of nine characters appointed by Elrond to accompany the Ring. Since leaving the Shire, the four hobbit friends have become inseparable, but among the other five travelers chosen by Elrond—the men Aragorn and Boromir, the dwarf Gimli, the elf Legolas, and Gandalf, a wizard—Boromir never really becomes part of the group of friends. When it comes to Gandalf, the situation is quite the opposite: through several hundred pages, we the readers are convinced that Gandalf has been killed in Moria, but he is brought to Lorien by Galadriel just as the brotherhood departs.

The Fellowship of the Ring can be viewed as one entity: a symbol of the Anthropos archetype, the dynamic principle of the collective individuation process of humankind. Jung stressed the strong connection between this particular archetype and quaternities and double quaternities.

It is a paradox that because of Boromir's betrayal, the Fellowship is broken up, but the friendships in the true brotherhood are deeply strengthened, and smaller groups of travelers act synchronistically, until all of the eight members are united in Minas Tirith after the victory. The archetype of the Anthropos or the brotherhood-on-the-quest denotes the collective process of individuation.

A typical male fairy-tale pattern begins: "Once upon a time, there was a king who had three sons." At the end of the tale, the youngest son has typically won his bride and half of the kingdom. So the joyful new era cannot commence until Aragorn has celebrated his wedding to Arwen. By the time Gandalf and Frodo leave Middle-earth two years later, yet another member of the brotherhood has married: Sam and Rosa have wed, thereby adding a female character to the Royal Quaternio and to the hobbit quaternio. At this time, the Fourth Era, the Era of Man, commences.

The Lord of the Rings is a story that reflects the male psyche. But for many reasons, it is not at all difficult for women to identify themselves with the characters. Although there are not many female figures in the book, values often regarded as being feminine are highly esteemed. Green nature and a holistic worldview are contrasted to the black, barren, poisoned nature and a mechanistic worldview; compassionate relationships stand in contrast to cold intellectualism; and serving the community is in contrast to the lust for power. Galadriel rules at the center of Middle-earth and might be interpreted as the feminine aspect of the Self, as well as representing the Anima archetype. The shield maiden Éowyn, who slays the Nazgûl captain, is a strong heroine figure. Frodo and Sam possess feminine traits; their devoted friendship allows them to kiss, to embrace, and to fall asleep holding hands.

The inner and outer journeys are closely connected to each other. The fact that *The Lord of the Rings* contains a map is not an expression of Tolkien's pedantry. In the landscapes, we meet archetypes of transformation; they are not personified, but turn up in typical situations, locations, and ways and means. When we are taught the subject of geography at school or when we look up a location in a lexicon, we are first and foremost presented with quantitative information. The country we have looked up spans x number square miles, has x number of inhabitants, and a gross domestic product in the amount of x. All the information that we can look up is based on numbers. In contrast to this, Middle-earth is all charged with meaning; when Frodo climbs Amon Hen in his hour of destiny, Tolkien doesn't inform us of the height of the mountain in meters; instead, he describes the Seat of Seeing, the Hill of the Eye of the Men of Númenor.

Crossing a river is an irreversible choice. Entering mysterious forests always leads deeper into the unconscious, where there is magical help to be found. In order to reach a greater goal, a dangerous descent either to the kingdom of death or down a dark and hidden path is necessary. Other typical and impersonal traits belong to the characteristics of the Self, especially the mandala elements. These are circular formations, often divided into fourths or eighths or inscribed in a square, with the center in the shape of the sun, a star, a flower, a wheel, or an eye, often with a rotation or a spiral movement. Within the mandala, squares of circular architecture—for example, a castle, a city, or rows of tall trees reaching out from the centere like rays of the sun— are also symbols related to the Self. Before the hobbits are allowed to enter Galadriel's city or Minas Tirith, a symbolic circumambulation must take place. In *The Lord of the Rings*, we are presented with all of these symbols time and again.

The Shire itself is split up into quarters, and Tolkien has described the royal city, the Entmoot, and the city of Galadhrim in detail; they are all built in the structure of a mandala.

The forests are full of hidden resources, but like electric sparks, evil is generated from tower to tower. Frodo is fatally traumatized at the ruin of Weathertop; Saruman's tower, Isengard, is a perverted and degenerate place, and from the Dark Tower, Sauron's terrifying, lidless eye looks out, searching this way and that for his ring. Even Minas Tirith is threatened by Lord Denethor's lust for power and, finally, by his madness. When the armies of Aragorn and the Riders of Rohan approach the besieged Minas Tirith, a moment of *kairos* takes place: the wind turns after three days and three nights during which the world has seen nothing but shadow; the rooster crows at dawn, and light conquers darkness. On the very same day, Frodo and Sam succeed in escaping from the tower at Minas Morgul, and they commence on their pilgrimage to Mount Doom.

The geography of Middle-earth consists of an emotional and mental landscape, determined by its inner meaning. The ancient, mythological worldview has long been lost by the Western world, but a similar universe has been re-created by Tolkien in an entirely new and psychological way. The importance of Tolkien's emphasis on the value and reality of the inner, archetypal world cannot be overestimated.

It has often been stated that originally Tolkien had wanted to create a mythology for England. But what does that actually mean? According to Tom Shippey (2000, p. xv), one of Tolkien's important sources of inspiration was the Danish poet, visionary, theologian, and philologist, N. F. S. Grundtvig. What Grundtvig succeeded in doing in the previous century in Denmark with his passionate interest in the sagas and epic literature was nothing less than re-creating the Danish national identity. He published several volumes of Nordic mythology and epic literature, but more important, through his lectures, speeches, and sermons all over Denmark, he became extremely influential, a spiritual giant in the history of Denmark.

As Shippey explains, "Nicolai Grundtvig, the Dane, insisted on the concept of *levende ord*, 'the living word.' It is not enough for the philologist, the 'word-lover,' to be scholarly. The scholar also has to transmit his results into the life and speech and imagination of the greater world" (2000, p. xxxiv).

Another link between Tolkien and Grundtvig is the epic poem, *Beowulf*. The manuscript of the poem can be dated back to approximately the year 1000; its story takes place in the elder days of a royal court in Denmark that is very similar to the Golden Hall of King Théoden in *The Lord of the Rings*. Translating *Beowulf* into Danish as early as 1820, Grundtvig the philologist was actually the first scholar of *Beowulf*, and his detailed knowledge of Old English would make him a kindred spirit to Tolkien and his famous 1936 essay on *Beowulf*.

But the affinity between Grundtvig and Tolkien goes deeper. In literature on Tolkien's work, it is often discussed at length why Tolkien always insisted that his trilogy was "a fundamentally religious and Catholic work," which in his own opinion would explain why he had removed "practically all references to anything like 'religion,' to cults or practices, in the imaginary world" (quoted in Shippey 2000, p. 175). How could there be any religious meaning in *The Lord of the Rings*, when the tale takes place in a seemingly pagan world and God is not mentioned? Shippey, for one, is inclined to disagree with Tolkien's own statements (ibid., p. 174).

Danish culture as a whole has been profoundly influenced by Grundtvig the theologian, and to many Danes a severance of the pagan world from the Christian world would simply seem unnatural. Pastor Grundtvig maintained that man has divine status simply by being created in the image of God, even without professing to the Christian faith.

On the background of this belief, Grundtvig the visionary formulated his agenda: a "school for life," which materialized in the second half of the nineteenth century when Grundtvigian *højskoler* ("folk schools") and Free Schools were built all over Denmark. In these schools, reading, retelling, and studying Nordic mythology, sagas, epic poems, and folk tales was—and is to this day—an essential part of the syllabus. Christian teachings, however, were not. On the other hand, in Denmark in the 1950s, before the hippies discovered it, *The Lord of the Rings* was actually only read by Christian circles. Even today, I know many Danish parsons who love *The Lord of the Rings*, and one parson who even published a book on the biblical motives in *The Lord of the Rings* to be used as teaching material when preparing young people for confirmation (Tjalve 2002). So, when Tolkien wrote that "the religious element is absorbed into the story and the symbolism," it seems perfectly logical from the Grundtvigian point of view (quoted in Shippey 2000, p. 175).

1   FÆRY OR THE COLLECTIVE UNCONSCIOUS

As stated above, I do not believe it essential whether Tolkien knew anything of Jung. Much more interesting is the fact that Tolkien's Faëry and Jung's collective unconscious independently seem to point toward the same area of the human mind.

In his essay on fairy-stories, Tolkien described "the Perilous Realm," which he also named "Faëry." According to Tolkien, both fairy tales and the legends of the Grail belonged to this realm, which did *not* include books like *Winnie-the-Pooh* or *Alice in Wonderland*. To Tolkien, magic and mythology came from this layer of fantasy, and fairy-stories were especially able to offer fantasy, recovery, escapism, and consolation. Jung wrote in his memoir:

> The stories of the Grail had been of the greatest importance to me ever since I read them, at the age of fifteen, for the first time. I had an inkling that a great secret still lay hidden behind those stories . . . . My whole being was seeking for something still unknown which might confer meaning upon the banality of life. (1979, p. 189)

What Jung in his early years called the "great secret" was later named the "collective unconscious," signifying the layer of the unconscious structured by the archetypes. During World War I, while Tolkien was sitting in the trenches working on his first attempts at inventing the language and mythology of elves, Jung was busy drawing mandalas and experiencing visions and fantasies, which he carefully recorded: "First I formulated the things as I had observed them, usually in the 'high-flown language,' for that corresponds to the style of the archetypes. Archetypes speak the language of high rhetoric, even of bombast" (1979, pp. 201-2). Jung was not comfortable with this bombastic style of rhetoric; it was as unpleasant to him as fingernails on a chalkboard. In spite of this, he took his visions seriously; he even transferred his fantasies to *The Red Book*, which he also illustrated beautifully. Jung's experiments were an attempt at aesthetic or artistic expression, the path that Tolkien finally took, while Jung utilized his fantasies as a basis for creating psychological theories.

The archaic and humorless style in Tolkien's *Silmarillion* is similar to the style of the archetypes. It is a style often found in the products of active imagination, a visualization technique which Jung developed. Tolkien invented a similar method for transforming psychological material into fantasies; he called his method escapism and described to his son, Christopher, how he had discovered the power of imagination:

> I took to "Escapism"; or really transforming
> experience into another form and symbol with
> Morgoth and Orcs and the Eldare (representing
> beauty and grace of life and artefact) and so on; and it

has stood me in good stead in many hard years since, and I still draw on the conceptions then hammered out. (*Letters*, no. 73)

While Tolkien enjoyed his fantasies and let himself be inspired and encouraged by them, Jung had more ambivalent feelings about his fantasies; as a psychiatrist, he associated mythological fantasies with psychosis. Only gradually did he come to view active imagination as a useful and healing technique. In retrospect, Jung came to almost the same conclusions as Tolkien:

The years when I was pursuing my inner images were the most important in my life—in them everything essential was decided. It all began then; the later details are only supplements and clarifications of the material that burst forth from the unconscious, and at first swamped me. It was the *prima materia* for a lifetime's work. (1961b, p. 199)

Both Jung and Tolkien were convinced that mankind is in a crucial dilemma, and that transformation must come from the inner man. In 1957, Jung commented on this:

As at the beginning of the Christian Era, so again today we are faced with the problem of the general moral backwardness which has failed to keep pace with our scientific, technical, and social progress. So much is at stake and so much depends on the psychological constitution of modern man. Is he capable of resisting the temptation to use his power for the purpose of staging a world conflagration? Is he conscious of the path he is treading, and what the conclusions are that must be drawn from the present world situation and his own psychic situation? Does he know that he is on the point of losing the life-preserving myth of the inner man which Christianity has treasured up for him? Does he realize what lies in store should this catastrophe ever befall him? Is he even capable of realizing that this would in fact be a catastrophe? And finally, does the individual know that *he* is the makeweight that tips the scales? (1957, par. 586)

Tolkien had his characters express similar considerations during the discussions on the Ring and the fate of Middle-earth at Elrond's council. Elrond had clearly told Boromir that the Ring of Power could not be used as a weapon in the service of good; only someone already possessing great powers would be able to wield the Ring according to his will, but this would place his soul in mortal danger, soon transforming him into a new Dark Lord. The only solution was to destroy the Ring in the fire of Mount Doom. Erestor asked the council if it would even be possible to locate the fire; he feared that the solution of destroying the Ring would turn out to be a path of despair or folly.

"Despair, or folly?" said Gandalf. "It is not despair, for despair is only for those who see the end beyond all doubt. We do not. It is wisdom to recognize necessity, when all other courses have been weighed, though as folly it may appear to those who cling to false hope. Well, let folly be our cloak, a veil before the eyes of the Enemy! For he is very wise, and weighs all things to a nicety in the scales of his malice. But the only measure that he knows is desire, desire for power; and so he judges all hearts. Into his heart the thought will not enter that any will refuse it, that having the Ring we may seek to destroy it. If we seek this, we shall put him out of reckoning."

"At least for a while," said Elrond. "The road must be trod, but it will be very hard. And neither strength nor wisdom will carry us far upon it. This quest may be attempted by the weak with as much hope as the strong. Yet such is oft the course of deeds that move the wheels of the world: small hands do them because they must, while the eyes of the great are elsewhere." (1:282–83)

In 1957, Jung wrote that confronting the shadow is not solely a negative experience (1957, par. 582). Through self-knowledge we come upon the inner world of imagery, which contains great dynamic power. Whether the activation of these forces will tend toward construction or catastrophe depends entirely on the attitude and capacity of the conscious mind.

Tolkien had a concept for this construction: he called it "Eucatastrophe," and a main theme in *The Lord of the Rings* is unmistakably the confrontation with the shadow. So how can this transformation come to pass? The spiritual transformation of humankind cannot take place from one generation to the next. Jung had modest expectations of the influence of psychotherapy, but he described how an individual with insight into his or her own actions, and therefore access to his or her unconscious, has an influence on others. This influence does not work through persuasion or preaching, but takes place spontaneously and involuntarily.

Another factor to be reckoned with is the unconscious *Zeitgeist*, the spirit of the present, which compensates for our conscious opinions and precipitates changes that are yet to take place. Great art is often an expression of this *Zeitgeist*. Jung felt, however, that an essential factor was missing in contemporary art: "Certainly art, so far as we can judge of it, has not yet discovered in this darkness what it is that could hold all men together and give expression to their psychic wholeness" (1957, par. 584). Jung continued on to explain that, in his view, art must be an expression of the collective unconscious:

> Great art till now has always derived its fruitfulness
> from myth, from the unconscious process of
> symbolization which continues through the ages and,
> as the primordial manifestation of the human spirit,
> will continue to be the root of all creation in the
> future . . . We are living in what the Greeks called the
> *kairos*—the right moment—for a "metamorphosis of
> the gods," of the fundamental principles and symbols.
> This peculiarity of our time, which is certainly
> not of our conscious choosing, is the expression of
> the unconscious man within us who is changing.
> Coming generations will have to take account of this
> momentous transformation if humanity is not to
> destroy itself through the might of its own technology
> and science. (1957, par. 585)

Only a few years before Jung expressed these thoughts, *The Lord of the Rings* had been published, and in my opinion, Tolkien succeeded in creating precisely what Jung had felt was missing in modern art. Furthermore, *The Lord of the Rings* describes the transition from one era to the next; this is a metamorphosis of the gods, where the old world must perish so that a new world may be resurrected. We mustn't be fooled by the fact that the tale apparently takes place in an undefined mythical past; all the appendixes, all the chronology and mythological background in the *Silmarillion* form the longest "Once upon a time" in the world.

In *The Lord of the Rings*, we are beyond time and space. As readers, we have been transported to a psychological universe, to the world of dreams and fantasies, to the vast kingdom of the collective psyche. Tolkien associated evil with darkness and void, goodness with light and the land of the living. In addition to darkness and void, the shadow is also characterized by terror, apathy, and despair, all psychological conditions. There is, however, no sharp division between inner and outer worlds. When Sauron is gaining strength, this is directly visible in the landscape, because at the same time, the shadow is increasing.

Although Tolkien is not expressing himself in a psychological way, he does insist that fantasy is a legitimate part of human nature:

> The realm of fairy-story is wide and deep and high
> and filled with many things: all manner of beasts
> and birds are found there; shoreless seas and stars

uncounted; beauty that is an enchantment, and an ever-present peril; both joy and sorrow as sharp as swords. In that realm a man may, perhaps, count himself fortunate to have wandered, but its very richness and strangeness tie the tongue of the traveler who would report them. And while he is there it is dangerous for him to ask too many questions, lest the gates should be shut and the keys be lost. (1983, p. 109)

2 THE ARCHETYPE OF CONSCIOUSNESS: THE HOBBITS

In 1930, Tolkien gave a lecture entitled "A Secret Vice," discoursing about the value of invented languages. At that time, he was busy creating his mythology and his elvish languages. He asked his audience to bear with him, since these matters had only been created for personal use and enjoyment: "It's just a hobby" (1983, p. 3).[1] Some time later, Tolkien was marking student essays, and suddenly, without knowing why, he scribbled, "In a hole in the ground there lived a hobbit"—the opening sentence of *The Hobbit*.

Understandably, there have been many speculations regarding the etymology of the word *hobbit*, since Tolkien was always so careful with his choice of words. But here, I simply suggest that the hob*bit* is the spontaneous personification of Tolkien's hob*by*. The hobbit is the unexpected fruit of a synthesis between Tolkien's conscious and long-standing work on his invented languages and mythology and a creative reaction from his unconscious. Without the hobbits and their mediating function, there would simply never have been a story to tell. Hobbits represent essential human qualities which influence their environment wherever they go.

By the time we have read Tolkien's foreword to *The Lord of the Rings*, a long prologue entitled "Concerning Hobbits, and other matters," and seventeen uneventful years following Bilbo's birthday party have passed, Frodo has turned fifty, Sam thirty-five, Merry thirty-two, and Pippin twenty-eight. Hobbits are not considered to be adults until the age of thirty-three, and they often live to be one hundred years old.

Each of the four hobbits has his own goal of individuation within the trilogy: Pippin and Merry are transformed from young boys to men, Sam develops from a young man to a mature individual with the capacity to marry and have a family, and finally, Frodo experiences a midlife crisis, culminating in an acceptance of mortality. These three stages are aspects of an archetypal Ego model, with Frodo as the dominating figure at the beginning of the tale.

Each of the hobbits has a numinous experience, which activates the beginning of their individuation process. For Frodo, this happens as he comes to understand the special qualities of the Ring. Sam's individuation process is activated by his first encounter with the elves. Meeting Treebeard is decisive for Merry and Pippin. In each case, a special contact with a symbol of the self alters the consciousness of the hobbits.

In volume one, all of the events are experienced through the eyes of Frodo, from the birthday party during which Bilbo leaves the scene, to the last pages, wherein Sam follows Frodo across the River of Anduin. In volume two, the Fellowship is broken up, first into three, then into four groups, and ego-consciousness is now shared between all four hobbits. Sam's consciousness becomes active and begins to alternate with Frodo's consciousness, and on the long journey to Mordor, we increasingly follow Sam's thoughts and feelings and his observations of the suffering that Frodo is going through. At the end of volume two, after the dramatic battle with the giant monster spider, Shelob, Sam's consciousness takes over definitively. By volume three, we no longer experience the story from the inside of Frodo's mind.

Remarkably often, a chapter or a passage ends when one of the hobbits falls asleep or loses consciousness and/or a new chapter begins with one of them waking up to a new situation. Old Man Willow casts a sleeping spell on Frodo, and later he is overpowered by the Barrow-wight: "Then a grip stronger and colder than iron seized him. The icy touch froze his bones, and he remembered no more" (1:151). He also loses consciousness while confronting the Black Rider on Weathertop on the 6th of October: "At the same time he struck at the feet of his enemy. A shrill cry rang out in the night; and he felt a pain like a dart of poisoned ice pierce his left shoulder" (1:208). Again, after crossing the ford at Rivendell: "Then Frodo felt himself falling, and the roaring and confusion seemed to rise and engulf him together with his enemies. He heard and saw no more" (1:227).

This ends book 1, and book 2 opens with Frodo waking up comfortably in the House of Elrond. Here, he experiences a far more pleasant version of the dissolution of consciousness after a banquet in honor of his own healing. When the meal is finished, the party retires to the Hall of Fire, where the elves sing and play:

At first the beauty of the melodies and of the interwoven words in elven-tongues, even though he understood them little, held him in a spell, as soon as he began to attend to them. Almost it seemed that the words took shape, and visions of far lands and bright things that he had never yet imagined opened out before him; and the firelit hall became like a golden mist above seas of foam that sighed upon the margins of the world. Then the enchantment became more and more dreamlike, until he felt that an endless river of swelling gold and silver was flowing over him, too multitudinous for its pattern to be comprehended; it became part of the throbbing air about him, and it drenched and drowned him. Swiftly he sank under its shining weight into a deep realm of sleep. (1:245–46)

Bilbo explains to Frodo that staying awake in the Hall of Fire can be difficult, until you get used to it (1:250). Here, Tolkien is describing a psychological state wherein consciousness approaches deep layers of the unconscious and its imagery-forming activity, which is so similar to the state of dreaming that Frodo falls asleep.

By the time Frodo is struck unconscious by the sting of Shelob at the end of volume two, the reader no longer experiences this attack from the inside of Frodo's mind. In volumes two and three, other parts of ego-consciousness either wake up or lose consciousness on important thresholds.

The consciousness of Pippin wakes up in the scene where Merry and he are carried away by orcs (2:47). Merry faints in Minas Tirith following his confrontation with the Nazgûl king: "Help me, Pippin! It's all going dark again, and my arm is so cold" (3:135). Pippin faints, looking into the palantir:

> Suddenly the lights went out. He gave a gasp and
> struggled; but he remained bent, clasping the ball
> with both hands. Closer and closer he bent, and
> then became rigid; his lips moved soundlessly for
> a while. Then with a strangled cry he fell back and
> lay still. (2:197)

And once more, on the Morannon field during the last battle: "Blackness and stench and crushing pain came upon Pippin, and his mind fell away into a great darkness. . . . And his thought fled far away and his eyes saw no more" (3:169).

Sam is the last to wake up. Hurling himself against the gates to the Tower of Cirith Ungol at the end of book 4, he is struck senseless and doesn't wake up until opening of book 6: "Sam roused himself painfully from the ground. For a moment he wondered where he was, and then all the misery and despair returned to him" (3:173). This is a miserable moment for Sam, but later it is Sam who wakes up to joy and delight in the land of Ithilien, under the green beech trees (3:229).

The hobbits tend to lose consciousness when the story has reached a point of no return, a situation where the plot is apparently stuck, while awakenings set a new scene. The pattern described above is so striking that I feel it reveals how Tolkien wrestled with his story. According to Tom Shippey, Tolkien struggled along with his hobbits for many years. The final version of *The Lord of the Rings* as we know it is very different from the many drafts that Tolkien worked out. For example, when the Riders of Rohan suddenly appear on the plain, it seems just as surprising to the author's mind as to his readers. This is a way of writing that strongly resembles active imagination, the dreamlike but conscious state wherein the unconscious is allowed to become active and conscious and critical reflection is not applied until later, which is the way Tolkien described the realm of fairy-story: "And while he is there it is dangerous for him to ask too many questions, lest the gates should be shut and the keys be lost" (1983, p. 109).

One way to look at the hobbits as an ego-model is to use Jung's psychological typology. Consciousness is primarily oriented by four basic psychological functions: thinking, feeling, sensation, and intuition. All four functions are to be found in every human being, but Jung felt that one of these functions would normally be more differentiated and conscious, two of the functions could become partially conscious, while the fourth function would always remain unintegrated and primarily unconscious.

The four hobbits could represent the four psychological functions: thinking (Frodo), intuition (Pippin), sensation (Merry), and feeling (Sam). If we now view the waking-up-and-falling-asleep sequences from this angle, we see that the introverted thinking function is dominant in the beginning, and after some time the extraverted intuition function and to some extent the sensation function become active. This sequence is to be expected in the normal course of psychological development, where consciousness is integrating formerly unconscious contents. The first and most differentiated function will be supplemented by the second and third. But then something very unexpected happens:

the feeling function (Sam), which represents the fourth and therefore normally the most unconscious function, in the end becomes dominant in the "hobbit-consciousness," while the thinking function disappears altogether into the collective unconscious as Frodo sails away from Middle-earth.

In my clinical experience, such a pattern only occurs if the man in question was naturally disposed as a feeling type. However, in Western societies, there always was—and to this day still is—a strong pressure on boys to adapt to the "normal" masculine gender role. A boy disposed as a feeling type, that is, who is oriented toward values and relationships, will automatically be pushed in the opposite typological direction. If, in addition, he loves books and words and is highly intelligent, he will be perceived as a thinking type and may well end up as a professor in Old English at Oxford, although even there, he does not really "fit in."[2]

To man like this, it may happen—as it often does during an analysis—that later in life the repressed feeling function, which is related to his most healthy and creative qualities, will emerge during the individuation process. This is what seems to have happened to J. R. R. Tolkien as he traveled along with his hobbits for many long years, and his travail resulted in a wonderful gift to us all—*The Lord of the Rings*.

FRODO

That fateful spring, seventeen years after Bilbo's birthday party, when Gandalf reappears, it is to tell Frodo what he has discovered about his ring. Frodo understands intuitively that his task is quite different than the adventure his uncle Bilbo took on:

> "For where am I to go? And by what shall I steer? What is to be my quest? Bilbo went to find a treasure, there and back again; but I go to lose one, and not return, as far as I can see." (1:75)

Frodo is summarizing a typical hero pattern, and he is correct in estimating his own fate. For Frodo, everything is in contrast to this pattern. Frodo goes reluctantly, and he meets no princess nor wins any kingdom.

Frodo sighed:

> "I should like to save the Shire, if I could— though there have been times when I thought the inhabitants too stupid and dull for words, and have felt that an earthquake or an invasion of dragons might be good for them. But I don't feel like that now. I feel that as long as the Shire lies behind, safe and comfortable, I shall find wandering more bearable: I shall know that somewhere there is a firm foothold, even if my feet cannot stand there again. . . . And I suppose I must go alone, if I am to do that and save the Shire." (1:71–72)

Frodo is, by hobbit standards, an eccentric dreamer—but what he has just heard absolutely equals an invasion of dragons; something he cannot fathom but which he has to react to. His perspective, however, is still very narrow. He does think beyond himself, but his consciousness does not embrace anything wider than the Shire. And yet, he suddenly feels a desire to see Bilbo again, a wish so strong that it conquers his fear. This urge to run out, to take to the road, is a few minutes later personified by the young Sam, who does not yet know fear. And some time later, the two even younger relatives, Merry and Pippin, appear, and they can be viewed as another expansion of the conscious resources.

This urge described by Tolkien is a complex one and cannot be identified simply as love for adventure, since it is mixed with sadness and fear of the unknown. There is no English word for it; in Danish, we call it *udve*, a combination of *ud*, meaning "out," and *ve*, as in birth pains. In fairy tales, it marks the stage at which the hero or heroine becomes active (Skogemann 2001, p. 38).

As we shall see, while the three younger hobbits all follow a normal, healthy track of development and maturation, Frodo breaks down in a physical sense although he grows in a spiritual way. He becomes the part that is sacrificing itself in the service of the emerging wholeness. Frodo's special development is already predicted during the hobbits stay in the house of Tom Bombadil and Goldberry.

For Frodo, the meeting with this strange and wonderful couple amounts to an experience with a positive self image, and it moves him deeply and personally. For the first time, he really grasps that something greater and deeper than the Shire exists in the world; yes, even Frodo's own small world is not what everything is about.

That night, Frodo has a dream about a man standing on the top of a tower. The man lifts his staff and is carried away by a giant eagle (1:138). The dream can be interpreted in a symbolic way—both the eagle and the wizard can be seen as symbols of transcendence, images that represent the beginning of individuation. Joseph Henderson connects the release through transcendence with the theme of the lonely journey or pilgrimage on which the initiate becomes acquainted with the nature of death: "But this is not death as a last judgment or other initiatory trial of strength; it is a journey of release, renunciation, and atonement, presided over and fostered by some spirit of compassion" (in Jung 1972, p. 152). This spirit, according to Henderson, is more often personified by a mistress rather than a master of initiation. The dream, of course, is also a true dream about Gandalf, who was a prisoner in Saruman's tower, Orthanc, and escaped on the back of the eagle.

The next night Frodo, in his dream, heard

> a sweet singing running in his mind: a song that
> seemed to come like a pale light behind a grey rain-
> curtain, and growing stronger to turn the veil all to
> glass and silver, until at last it was rolled back, and a
> far green country opened before him under a swift
> sunrise. (1:146)

This dream becomes real at the very end of the story as Frodo sails out into the West on his last journey, to Valinor, the Island of the Valar:

> And then it seemed to him that as in his dream in the
> house of Bombadil, the grey rain-curtain turned all to
> silver glass and was rolled back, and he beheld white
> shores and beyond them a far green country under a
> swift sunrise. (3:310)

When Frodo wakes up in Bombadil's house, "there was Tom whistling like a tree-full of birds; and the sun was already slanting down the hill and through the open window. Outside everything was green and pale gold" (1:146).

Suddenly the faraway Valinor is similar to Tom's house: the first and the last are connected. A light of hope is perceived at the end of the long, dark journey. The Island of the Valar is the strongest symbol of transcendence in the universe of *The Lord of the Rings*—the dwelling place of the godlike creators of Middle-earth, to where the elves may sail over the western sea, but where no mortal creature can go. In Frodo's very first dream, he is ascending the tall elf-tower beyond the western marches of the Shire, from the top of which one can see the sea—that is, in the direction of Valinor. Valinor is from the beginning the goal of Frodo's pilgrimage, death and immortality in one symbol.

But Frodo's journey has just begun. The same day, after leaving Tom's house, the hobbits get lost in a fog and become bewitched by the Barrow-wight. Frodo wakes up inside the barrow while the other hobbits, in a deathlike condition, are lying dressed up in white and adorned with gold and jewels. An incantation begins, evoking a world without sun, moon, or stars and dominated by a dark lord (1:152). We are not told why Frodo is not spellbound to the same extent as the other hobbits, but the obvious reason is that the Ring protects him. Frodo is, however, put to an ethical test. He could run off, and even Gandalf would agree that there was nothing else to do—Frodo thinks.

Psychologically, this is a dangerous confrontation with the collective unconscious, which is threatening to darken all consciousness. In the last moment, Frodo remembers the house down under the hill and Tom Bombadil. Tom had taught the hobbits a rhyme to sing if they were in need; the fog had made Frodo forget it, but now he calls out. Tom, of course, is also an archetypal figure (see chapter 4), but he represents those forces in the unconscious that support the growth of consciousness. Tom appears immediately; he sings the Barrow-wight away and restores the three hobbits to life again. Their own clothes have disappeared, but Tom says: "You've found yourselves again, out of the deep water. Clothes are but little loss, if you escape from drowning" (1:155).

The rebirth symbolism is obvious. The hobbits have been victims of an archetypal possession, to the extent that Merry even in coming back to his senses is still identified with the warrior who died by a spear in his heart.

Now Tom induces historical consciousness into the hobbits by telling them about the battle between the men from Westernesse (the ancestors of Aragorn) and the Witch King in Angmar a thousand years earlier. The hobbits don't understand what he is talking about, but they envision tall, grim men with bright swords. At this point, Tom equips the hobbits with daggers; much later Merry will wound this selfsame Witch King, now the captain of the Nazgûl, with this dagger. "Fighting had not before occurred to any of them as one of the adventures in which their flight would land them" (1:157).

Tom sees the hobbits safely to the border of his domain, and at the Prancing Pony in Bree, Aragorn takes over as guide and guardian. Here the Ring itself becomes active; it slips onto Frodo's finger without his conscious knowledge

(1:172–73). On Weathertop, when Frodo is attacked by the Nazgûl and puts on the Ring for the third time, it is described how the Ring works on the mind from within, akin to a narcotic addiction:

> The desire to do this [put on the Ring] laid hold of
> him, and he could think of nothing else. He did not
> forget the Barrow, nor the message of Gandalf; but
> something seemed to be compelling him to disregard
> all warnings, and he longed to yield. (1:207)

Frodo puts on the Ring and now he can see the Ring spirits—Ringwraiths—in "the other world." The Nazgûl king bears down on him with sword and knife and wounds him in the left shoulder. Although this evil wound will continue to hurt always, it also has another effect on Frodo. In Rivendell, while Frodo is recovering, Gandalf studies him with his wizard's eye and sees a change in Frodo, a hint of transparency:

> "Still that must be expected," said Gandalf to
> himself. "He is not half through yet, and to what he
> will come in the end not even Elrond can foretell. Not
> to evil, I think. He may become like a glass filled with
> a clear light for eyes to see that can." (1:235)

Not only Ringwraiths are present in the other world— the elves also have another spiritual shape, for example, the shining figure of white light Frodo saw at the ford, which was Glorfindel's spirit shape. So Frodo's transparency is a sign that he has come closer to the other world or, psychologically speaking, the world of the collective unconscious.

In the Council of Elrond, the story of the Ring is told by the involved parties. It appears that somebody has to take the Ring to Mordor to destroy it. Bilbo asks who that should be.

> No one answered. The noon-bell rang. Still no one spoke. Frodo glanced at all the faces, but they were not turned to him. All the Council sat with downcast eyes, as if in deep thought. A great dread fell on him, as if he was awaiting the pronouncement of some doom that he had long foreseen and vainly hoped might after all never be spoken. (1:284)

All the faces that do not turn toward Frodo create an intense feeling that it is exactly him they are all waiting for:

> An overwhelming longing to rest and remain at peace by Bilbo's side in Rivendell filled all his heart. At last with an effort he spoke, and wondered to hear his own words, as if some other will was using his small voice.
> "I will take the Ring," he said, "though I do not know the way." (1:284)

Elrond, like Gandalf, is convinced that Frodo is destined to be the Ring-bearer, although just in that nobody could have foreseen this. Psychologically, one may say that Frodo is in the same situation as any present-day person who realizes his or her total helplessness in solving the central spiritual problem of the world. That is, the ego is helpless, but at this point forces in the psyche are mobilized that far surpass the capabilities of the ego in the shape of the strong helping figures who will go with Frodo.

It is in the dark mines of Moria that the Ring begins to feel heavy, and at the same time the changes which have taken place in Frodo present themselves to his own consciousness for the first time:

> His senses were sharper and more aware of things
> that could not be seen. One sign of change that he
> soon had noticed was that he could see more in
> the dark than any of his companions, save perhaps
> Gandalf. (1:325)

Frodo begins to hear something almost inaudible. It is Gollum, who follows him like a shadow. In the psychological sense, Gollum is Frodo's shadow, that same being who Frodo thought should have been killed when he first was told about him and his connection with the Ring. Now, when Gollum is approaching, he just seems to be some kind of faraway evil, but he will not be shaken off again until the end of the story.

It is only during the stay in Lothlórien's golden elvish paradise that Gollum is made to wait outside; for there no evil is allowed entrance. Here Frodo meets Galadriel in her function as the mistress of initiation and individuation. In Galadriel's mirror Frodo sees the darkness and the void and then the image of his enemy, the terrifying Eye: "The Eye was rimmed with fire, but was itself glazed, yellow as a cat's, watchful and intent, and the black slit of its pupil opened on a pit, a window into nothing" (1:379).

When looking into a mirror, one sees oneself, and so the mirror is a common metaphor for self-reflection in the ordinary sense. But the magic water mirror of Galadriel shows parts of the self far away from consciousness. According to

Jung, water is the most common symbol for the unconscious. Water indicates spirit that has become unconscious (Jung 1954a, par. 40). One of Jung's patients, a Protestant theologian, often had the same dream: he stood on a mountain slope with a deep valley below and in it a dark lake; as he approached the shore, everything grew dark and uncanny, and a gust of wind suddenly rushed over the face of the water. He was seized by a panic fear and awoke (ibid., par. 34).

The magic water mirror constellates a border field where visions and revelations appear. The Swiss mystic and hermit, Saint Nicholas of Flüe, had a vision so overwhelming that it occupied him for the rest of his life. Originally, it was terrifying: "he himself used to say that he had seen a piercing light resembling a human face. At the sight of it he feared that his heart would burst into little pieces" (ibid., par. 13).

To the old Hebrews, the fear of God was self-evident. After Jacob had his famous dream about the ladder to heaven by which angels moved up and down and God had made him wonderful promises, he woke up and was very afraid. He said, "How dreadful *is* this place! this *is* none other but the house of God, and this *is* the gate of heaven" (Gen. 28:17).

Galadriel pulls Frodo back from his trancelike state; she knows what he has seen, and she assures him that the Dark Lord cannot penetrate her realm. At their departure the next day, Galadriel's parting gift for Frodo is a small crystal phial in which the light of Eärendil's star is caught (1:393). Here, Galadriel has given Frodo a gift to strengthen the spiritual light in himself which Gandalf already sensed in Rivendell. It is a truly magical thing that is opposed to the power of the

Ring. The light of Eärendil's star comes from the last of the three Silmarils, which Fëanor created from the light of the two trees in Valinor in the oldest days, and it is a symbol of hope for men and elves.

When Frodo slips on the Ring for the fourth time to escape the desire of Boromir, he runs to the summit of Amon Hen and sits down on the ancient Seat of Seeing. Everywhere there are signs of war of apocalyptic dimensions: he sees riders galloping across the grasslands of Rohan, and he sees the battlements of the white city, Minas Tirith. But then his gaze is drawn toward Mordor, Mount Doom, and the fortress of Sauron, Barad-dûr. Suddenly he feels the Eye as a finger groping for him.

Frodo is dangerously close to giving himself away when an inner voice commands him to take off the Ring. He regains consciousness and takes it off. The impact of the voice is such that, in that moment, he has conquered his fear of doing what he knows he must do. Still, Frodo believes that he has to travel alone. It is as though the pilgrimage symbol with the lonely pilgrim continues to be at work.

But Sam sees through his master's plan and throws himself into the river to grasp the boat with the invisible Frodo inside. For the first time, the solitary Frodo accepts a real mutual relation to another person. Very early in the story, Gandalf pointed out compassion and friendship as most important factors, and Sam personifies a loving spirit in relation to Frodo.

Together they cross the Anduin to walk in the Land of Shadows, and almost at once they get lost on the naked stone slopes of Emyn Muil. Frodo has from the beginning of the journey shown a tendency to lose his way and become overpowered by malicious magic powers that then, after all, must yield to stronger positive forces. However, after the experience with the mirror of Galadriel, he has gained insight and grown in his ability to meet his shadow instead of falling unconsciously into it. Now, instead of fleeing from the shadow, he makes contact with it: Frodo asks Gollum to be the hobbits' guide to Mordor, and he addresses him by his hobbit name, Sméagol. But Gollum says: "Don't ask Sméagol. Poor, poor, Sméagol, he went away long ago. They took his Precious, and he's lost now" (2:223).

Sméagol is the part of Gollum that represents his "hobbitness"—his, so to speak, human qualities. Sméagol is gone, he has been divested of his self. Gollum has been in possession of the Ring for centuries; it has left in him a void, an abysmal darkness. Gollum is also physically deformed by the Ring; he resembles an animal, an otterlike being. The Ring, his Precious, was his only preoccupation for all this time during which he was excluded from the hobbitlike community of which he was originally a part. So he is a collective hobbit shadow, the opposite of everything normal hobbits are. His long tenure in possession of the Ring is what makes Gollum the personal problem of Frodo—and Sam.

Gollum's search for roots and depths and secrets is completely without meaning or spirit. Thus, Gollum personifies a modern problem: the loss of meaning, or godlessness. Jung argues:

> Symbols are spirit from above, and under those
> conditions the spirit is above too. Therefore it would

be a foolish and senseless undertaking for such people to wish to experience or investigate an unconscious that contains nothing but the silent, undisturbed sway of nature. Our unconscious, on the other hand, hides living water, spirit that has become nature, and that is why it is disturbed. Heaven has become for us the cosmic space of the physicists, and the divine empyrean a fair memory of things that once were. (1954a, par. 50)

One cannot fish anything of value out of deep waters if one has fallen into them, that is, if one has become possessed by the unconscious. Gollum personifies the negative effect of the possession of the treasure that has possessed him. Now that Frodo has seen him in his misery, he is filled with pity, as Bilbo was before him, and at the same time he understands much more about the danger of giving in to the lure of the Ring.

Frodo truly needs Gollum, but he will not trust him unless Gollum can give a binding oath:

"Swear?" said Frodo.
"Sméagol," said Gollum suddenly and clearly, opening his eyes wide and staring at Frodo with a strange light. "Sméagol will swear on the Precious." (2:224)

Sam looks on, amazed, while Frodo seems to grow and Gollum shrinks:

. . . a tall stern shadow, a mighty lord who hid his brightness in grey cloud, and at his feet a little

whining dog. Yet the two were in some way akin
and not alien: they could reach one another's minds.
Gollum raised himself and began pawing at Frodo,
fawning at his knees.

"Down! down!" said Frodo. "Now speak your
promise!"

"We promises, yes I promise!" said Gollum. "I will
serve the master of the Precious. Good master, good
Sméagol." (2:225)

Frodo's mental contact with Sméagol calls forth the
remains of the hobbit nature in Gollum, for a time. When
they reach the entrance to Mordor itself through the lair
of the monster spider, Shelob, the connection is again
sundered. Frodo's fatal confrontation with Shelob has a
wholly other psychological meaning than Sam's fight with
her (see page 42):

. . . he was aware of eyes growing visible, two great
clusters of many-windowed eyes—the coming
menace was unmasked at last. The radiance of the
star-glass was broken and thrown back from their
thousand facets, but behind the glitter a pale deadly
fire began steadily to glow within, a flame kindled
in some deep pit of evil thought. Monstrous and
abominable eyes they were, bestial and yet filled with
purpose and with hideous delight, gloating over their
prey trapped beyond all hope of escape. (2:329–30)

Frodo goes forward with Galadriel's star-glass and his shining sword to meet the eyes.

No brightness so deadly had ever afflicted them before. From sun and moon and star they had been safe underground, but now a star had descended into the very earth. Still it approached, and the eyes began to quail. (2:330)

The many eyes point toward an archetypal motif: Shelob's eyes reveal an alien form of consciousness. The founder of the Jesuits, Ignatius Loyola, had a vision of a snake full of shining eyes. Jung thinks that such motives point to a "possibility that complexes possess a kind of consciousness, a luminosity of their own" (1955–56, par. 270). The star-spangled night sky is another related image, which is usually positive; here, the starlight is opposite the subterranean Shelob's many eyes representing the dangerous, overwhelming aspect of the unconscious—akin to a psychotic breakdown. Shelob's dangerousness is different from Sauron's single Eye; it is more archaic and instinctive. Shelob is a symbol of the Mother archetype in its most destructive aspect.

Frodo has a short-lived heroic moment when he has driven Shelob off and cut a way through the cobwebs, but then he carelessly runs on without looking back, and he is struck down from behind, stung by Shelob. In a deathlike state, Frodo is spun into a chrysalis in her sticky web for a later meal (2:336).

From a number of fairy tales, we know similar instances where a deathlike condition is inflicted by a dominant and negative female figure on the hero or heroine. Snow White in her glass coffin is probably the most well known; a similar motif is also present in the tales of Briar Rose and Amor and

Psyche. In dreams, giant spiders are frequently archetypal symbols of the evil mother; and Shelob is a particularly abominable example:

> Far and wide her lesser broods, bastards of the
> miserable mates, her own offspring, that she slew,
> spread from glen to glen . . . . But none could rival her,
> Shelob the Great, last child of Ungoliant to trouble
> the unhappy world. (2:332)

Here Tolkien adds repeated incest to Shelob's evil habits; Ungoliant, who is Shelob's own mother, was Melkor's female partner in evil in the oldest days. Shelob has a kind of partnership with Sauron, who calls her his cat and feeds her prisoners, but she owns him not (2:333).

As I discussed earlier, Frodo has several times before fallen into a trance or unconsciousness in the confrontation with archetypal figures, but the poisonous sting of Shelob is going to have the worst aftermath. Naked, he comes to himself in the upper chamber of the watchtower, and when Sam finds him, Frodo believes he has lost the Ring (3:187).

We have here a striking parallel to the scene where the three young hobbits came back naked from the bewitchment of the Barrow-wight, and to the scene where Gandalf returns naked to life after the fight with the Balrog (see page 63). There is also a rebirth motif in this scene, and one expects another substantial transformation in Frodo. This transformation equals a withdrawal from the world: apart from the intermezzo immediately following, the reader will have no further access to Frodo's anguish from the inside. However, this leaves the impression that his sufferings have become superhuman.

In this intermezzo, Sam fails to give back the Ring quickly enough, and he changes before Frodo's eyes into "a foul little creature with greedy eyes and slobbering mouth" (3:188). What we have here is a repetition of the situation in Rivendell when Bilbo asked Frodo to see the Ring once more:

> To his distress and amazement he found that he was
> no longer looking at Bilbo; a shadow seemed to have
> fallen between them, and through it he found himself
> eyeing a little wrinkled creature with a hungry face
> and bony groping hands. He felt a desire to strike him.
> . . . Bilbo looked quickly at Frodo's face and passed
> his hand across his eyes. "I understand now," he said.
> "Put it away! I am sorry: sorry you have come in for
> this burden: sorry about everything." (1:244)

At that time, the reader has to believe that it was solely the power of the Ring over *Bilbo*, which showed itself this way, as we had heard already how difficult it was for him to let it go. But Tolkien is very precise: *a shadow seemed to have fallen between them.* The shadow turns both ways. In Rivendell, Frodo was completely unconscious of his own shadow. This is no longer the case following the encounter with Shelob:

> "O Sam!" cried Frodo. "What have I said? What have
> I done? Forgive me! After all you have done. It is the
> horrible power of the Ring." (3:188)

From this point on, Sam is taking the lead. As they come closer to their goal, their sufferings increase:

> . . . the dreadful menace of the Power that waited, brooding in deep thought and sleepless malice behind the dark veil about its Throne. Nearer and nearer it drew, looming blacker, like the oncoming of a wall of night at the last end of the world. (3:212)

This is a description of wandering in the valley of death. It is a time of despair for both of them, but mostly so for Frodo:

> Sam guessed that among all their pains he bore the worst, the growing weight of the Ring, a burden on the body and a torment to his mind. Anxiously Sam had noted how his master's left hand would often be raised as if to ward off a blow, or to screen his shrinking eyes from a dreadful Eye that sought to look in them. And sometimes his right hand would creep to his breast, clutching, and then slowly, as the will recovered mastery, it would be withdrawn. (3:212–13)

One of the great allures of the Ring is that of immortality. When they finally reach the goal of the journey, the Crack of Doom, Frodo is not able to resist anymore. He asks Sam to hold his hands, and Sam takes him on his back. But in that moment Gollum attacks Sam and separates them. Frodo alone walks the final stretch into the heart of Sauron's kingdom, where all other powers are subdued. Not even Galadriel's phial is able to bring out a light here. And so instead of throwing the Ring into the fire, Frodo says: "I have come, . . . But I do not choose now to do what I came to do. I will not do this deed. The Ring is mine!" (3:223).

Gollum jumps Frodo, fights with him, and bites off the finger with the Ring. Then he stutters and falls in the abyss with his Precious. Thus it happens that Gollum actually becomes the agent of the destruction of the Ring. It is a strange example of the motif well known from fairy tales that something evil brings about good.

So the goal has been reached, but Frodo has lost a finger. A part of him is lost forever, and this manifests itself afterward in dark dreams and deep depressions that will not yield. But his compassion for and understanding of others who have fallen under the power of evil has grown immensely. The same Frodo who originally thought that Gollum deserved to die has ended up becoming totally pacifistic. During the scouring of the Shire, Frodo prevents Sam from killing Saruman. He speaks wisely, almost as Gandalf would have done:

> "He was great once, of a noble kind that we should
> not dare to raise our hands against. He is fallen, and
> his cure is beyond us; but I would still spare him, in
> the hope that he may find it."
>
> Saruman rose to his feet, and stared at Frodo.
> There was a strange look in his eyes of mingled
> wonder and respect and hatred. "You have grown,
> Halfling," he said, "Yes, you have grown very much.
> You are wise, and cruel. You have robbed my revenge
> of sweetness, and now I must go hence in bitterness,
> in debt to your mercy. I hate it and you! Well, I go

and I will trouble you no more. But do not expect
me to wish you health and long life. You will have
neither. But that is not my doing. I merely foretell."
(3:299)

It is true that Frodo will not be rewarded for his sacrifices
to his community. His reward is temporary access to Valinor
to be cured of his mental wounds, but psychologically this
means that he definitively disappears from consciousness,
the ultimate consequence of the gradual retreat as the story
progresses and the reader loses direct contact with Frodo's
consciousness. Accordingly, it is the other three hobbits that
renew life in the Shire.

SAM

The Lord of the Rings is related to fairy tales although they, taken
separately, are of course are much simpler. Tolkien held fairy
tales in high regard; to exile them to the children's rooms was
not only a misunderstanding but also a degradation which
had done great damage to the genre, he thought (1983, p.
129–30). This was not the ruling opinion in the 1930s and
for many years that followed, but Tolkien has been proved
right. The great fairy tales with princes and princesses,
dragons and magical helpers, which Danish folklorists call
trylleeventyr, that is, "wonder tales" (*Zaubermärchen*), were
originally told by grownup men and women to other adults,
although of course the children listened, too, when the tales
were told in the home. But when fairy tales were written out
and published, the publishers, such as the Grimm brothers,

addressed them to children, and they censored the stories accordingly.

Jungian analyst Marie-Louise von Franz, who published a number of books with interpretations of fairy tales, basically understands them as images of processes in the collective unconscious. She focuses on their healing qualities:

> Such stories are healing because they express life
> dreams and the compensatory processes in the
> collective unconscious that balance the one-sidedness,
> the sickness, the constant deviations of human
> consciousness. (1997, p. 20)

In fairy tales, it is often the case that the character who in the beginning is reckoned as the fool by everyone is the one who succeeds in the end. The hero of the fairy tale differs from the mythological hero—who, like Aragorn, is strong and unconquerable—in the sense that the fairy-tale hero's strongest property is that he has his heart in the right place.

Sam is just such a hero. His full first name, Samwise, means "fool." From the very beginning, during the preparations for Bilbo's birthday party, Sam's potential foolishness is discussed. His father the gaffer is exchanging gossip about Bilbo's speculated fortune with a group of hobbits, among them the miller:

> "But my lad Sam will know more about that. He's in
> and out of Bag End. Crazy about stories of the old
> days he is, and he listens to all Mr. Bilbo's tales. Mr.
> Bilbo has learned him his letters—meaning no harm,
> mark you, and I hope no harm will come of it.

"Elves and dragons! I says to him. *Cabbages and potatoes are better for me and you. Don't go getting mixed up in the business of your betters, or you'll land in trouble too big for you, I says to him."* (1:32)

Seventeen years later, when rumors about war and darkness far away are reaching the Shire, Sam himself is talking with the miller's son, Torben, about the possible truth of the strange stories. Sam believes them, but Torben claims that "I can hear fireside-tales and children's stories at home, if I want to" (1:53). Sam reports that his cousin has seen a Tree-man bigger than a tree beyond the North Moors and that he has heard that many elves are traveling west. But he is just laughed at.

The very same night, Gandalf reappears after nine years' absence (1:55). During Frodo's and Gandalf's serious talk about the Ring the next morning, Sam is caught listening from outside the window. He is not scolded, but Gandalf orders Sam to keep the secret and travel with Frodo, and Sam reacts "like a dog invited for a walk. 'Me go and see Elves and all! Hooray!' he shouted, and then burst into tears" (1:73).

At a first glance, Sam appears to be a naïve and childlike gardener's boy. But in fairy tales such a persona is often hiding a princely nature. Secretly, Sam has learned to read and write, and he has learned all he could from Bilbo, and in hiding, he listened to everything. All this has established a fertile ground inside him and planted seeds which have not yet sprouted. But Sam's first meeting with the elves marks a turning point. When the small group of hobbits meets the elves, they walk with them through the forest: "Sam walked along at Frodo's side, as if in a dream, with an expression on his face half of fear and half of astonished joy" (1:90). The next day, after the hobbits have spent the night with the elves, Sam could not then or ever since "describe in words, nor picture clearly to himself, what he felt or thought that night, though it remained in his memory as one of the chief events in his life" (1:92).

However, when Frodo decides to leave the Shire very soon and explains to Sam that the journey will be very dangerous, something from that night pops up in Sam's mind:

> "*Don't you leave him!* they said to me. *Leave him!* I said.
> *I never mean to. I am going with him, if he climbs to the Moon; and if any of those Black Riders try to stop him, they'll have Sam Gamgee to reckon with*, I said. They laughed." (1:96)

Surprisingly, it is the elves who have talked to Sam like that. Frodo asks whether Sam likes the elves?

> "They seem a bit above my likes and dislikes, so to speak, . . . It don't seem to matter what I think about them. They are quite different from what I expected—so old and young, and so gay and sad, as it were." (1:96)

Frodo is amazed by the change he feels in Sam. Such reflections do not seem to come from the Sam he has known. Yet, as though talking to a child, Frodo continues to ask if Sam still wants to leave the Shire, now when he already has met elves:

> "Yes, sir. I don't know how to say it, but after last night I feel different. I seem to see ahead, in a kind

of way. I know we are going to take a very long road, into darkness; but I know I can't turn back. It isn't to see Elves now, nor dragons, nor mountains, that I want—I don't rightly know what I want: but I have something to do before the end, and it lies ahead, not in the Shire. I must see it through, sir, if you understand me." (1:96)

Clearly, the elves have been able to see right through the fool persona and call forth the inner resources of Sam. Psychologically speaking, Sam has won a conscious relation to the archetype of the Self. The other hobbits have no idea about Sam's true qualities. When they reach Buckland and meet Merry, Pippin reveals to Frodo that they have conspired with Sam, but Pippin's remark shows little respect: "Sam is an excellent fellow, and would jump down a dragon's throat to save you, if he did not trip over his own feet" (1:114).

In reality, Sam is the one who saves all of their lives shortly after. The hobbits have lost their way in the Old Forest; it is hot and they all become very sleepy. Sam is the only one who keeps his head and is suspicious of the old willow tree:

He was worried. The afternoon was getting late, and he thought this sudden sleepiness uncanny. "There's more behind this than sun and warm air," he muttered to himself. "I don't like this great big tree. I don't trust it. Hark at it singing about sleep now! This won't do at all!" (1:128)

He runs off and finds Frodo sleeping with his head in the

water near the edge of the river, and he pulls him away from the immediate threat of drowning.

Gradually Sam's status grows among the other hobbits. On the way to Weathertop, Aragorn tells the history of the tower and how Elendil was standing there waiting for Gil-Galad. Merry asks who he was, and to their great amazement Sam strikes up an elven song about Gil-Galad in answer. The next time we hear about Sam's status is when the hobbits take a rest in the old troll forest and ask for a song. Frodo encourages Sam to sing, and Merry supports him: "'Come on, Sam!' said Merry, 'There's more stored in your head than you let on about'" (1:218). Sam sings a funny song about a troll, and afterward Pippin wants to know wherever he learned that.

> Sam muttered something inaudible. "It's out of his own head, of course," said Frodo. "I am learning a lot about Sam Gamgee on this journey. First he was a conspirator, now he's a jester. He'll end up by becoming a wizard—or a warrior!" (1:220)

Frodo shall be right about both before the end.

In Lórien, the Company is tested by Queen Galadriel, and they all see Sam blushing. Later, Pippin asks him why:

> "If you want to know, I felt as if I hadn't got nothing on, and I didn't like it. She seemed to be looking inside me and asking me what I would do if she gave me the chance of flying back home to the Shire to a nice little hole with—with a bit of garden of my own." (1:373)

By Sam's answer one can see that the test not only consists of the temptation to get away from the danger but also reveals the individual's deepest and strongest desire to their own consciousness as well as to Galadriel. While Boromir is confronted with his secret desire to have the Ring for himself, Sam has no greater longings for himself than to grow his garden. That longing is held in high regard by the Queen of the Forest, and at their departure, Galadriel gives Sam a very special gift:

> "For you little gardener and lover of trees," she said to
> Sam, "I have only a small gift." She put into his hand
> a little box of plain grey wood, unadorned save for
> a single silver rune upon the lid. "Here is set G for
> Galadriel," she said; "but also it may stand for garden
> in your tongue. In this box there is earth from my
> orchard, and such blessing as Galadriel has still to
> bestow is upon it. It will not keep you on your road,
> nor defend you against any peril; but if you keep it
> and see your home again at last, then perhaps it may
> reward you. Though you should find all barren and
> laid waste, there will be few gardens in Middle-earth
> that will bloom like your garden, if you sprinkle this
> earth there. Then you may remember Galadriel, and
> catch a glimpse far off of Lórien, that you have seen
> only in our winter. For our spring and our summer
> are gone by, and they will never be seen on earth
> again save in memory." (1:392)

Sam is undivided in his loyalty and love for Frodo; he sees his own part of the great task as taking care of his master so he can do his job. In the decisive hour when the Company is sundered and Frodo has suddenly disappeared, only Sam quite understands Frodo's mind, which is how he manages to catch the boat with the invisible Frodo and, despite his fear of water and his inability to swim, he throws himself into the river. As Frodo comes to understand that Sam is ready to prevent his going unless he is taken along, their relation shifts toward one of equals: "It is no good trying to escape you. But I'm glad, Sam. I cannot tell you how glad. Come along! It is plain that we were meant to go together" (1:423).

On the other side of the river, they take up company with Gollum, who swears loyalty to Frodo. From then on, we no longer experience the mind of Frodo from inside. Gollum becomes their guide, and in the marshes they are wholly in his hands (2:227). Sam only reluctantly accepts his co-servant, and he never trusts him. It is Sam who secretly witnesses the schizophrenic scene where Gollum talks with Sméagol (2:240–41), and he understands that he has assessed the danger from Gollum in a fashion much too simple. He merely feared that Gollum would eat them, if he got the chance. Now he realizes that Gollum feels the call of the Ring. "She might help," says Gollum, and Sam understands that Gollum has made plans to betray them. But he does not tell Frodo about the split Gollum/Sméagol, who he names to himself Slinker and Stinker, and he also hides his knowledge from Gollum. In one instance, when Gollum sees Frodo peacefully sleeping in Sam's lap, he is filled with tender feelings toward Frodo, and Tolkien hints that Gollum is almost changing his mind (2:323–24); but when Sam wakes up with a suspicious remark, the moment is over.

The whole attempt to find an entrance to Mordor is experienced through Sam's consciousness, even though Frodo is the master and still makes the decisions. But this changes decisively after the meeting with Shelob. Already in the dark tunnel, where Shelob is waiting unseen, Sam is the one to remember Galadriel's light. Frodo still has strength enough to threaten Shelob and to use Sting to get them through the cobwebs, but then Shelob attacks him from behind while Gollum jumps on Sam (2:335).

Frodo succumbs, while Sam fights successfully with Gollum, who runs away (see page 28). Next, Sam sees Frodo lying lifeless with Shelob stooping over him. He jumps forward with a howl and grasps Sting in his left hand and starts fighting the monster, shoring away a claw from her foot. Then he springs in between her legs and wounds her, though not fatally.

> Now splaying her legs she drove her large bulk down
> on him again. Too soon. For Sam still stood upon his
> feet, and dropping his own sword, with both hands
> he held the elven-blade point upwards, fending off
> that ghastly roof; and so Shelob, with the driving
> force of her own cruel will, with strength greater
> than any warrior's hand, thrust herself upon a bitter
> spike. (2:338)

As Shelob is preparing herself for a fatal attack on Sam, he grips the phial of light from Galadriel and calls out her name, then he hears elves singing and he cries out, in an elven language that he does not know (here also rendered in English), a prayer to the goddess Varda:

A Elbereth Gilthoniel
o menel palan-diriel,
le nallon sí di'nguruthos!
A tiro nin, Fanuilos!

[O Elbereth Star-kindler,
From heaven gazing afar,
To thee I cry now in the shadow of death.
O look towards me, Everwhite!] (2:339)

The glass blazes like a white torch and the light scores Shelob's head with pain as it spreads from eye to eye. Shelob is defeated by Sam, who has revealed his indomitable spirit.

The fight against the dragon or some other monster is a widespread motive in myth and fairy tale. The mythological hero may have supernatural strength, but the fairy-tale hero has magic helpers, like Sam. In a Jungian interpretation, we understand this scene as the young man conquering the negative Mother archetype. Tolkien's description of Shelob wounding her abdomen on Sam's sword is an almost too obvious image of female genitals perceived as a stinking, poisonous, and deadly enemy to man. In a psychological sense, Sam conquers the archetypal fear of woman.

Still, the greatest task lies ahead. Frodo seems to be dead. What is Sam to do?

"What? Me, alone, go to the Crack of Doom
and all?" He quailed still, but the resolve grew.

"What? *Me* take the Ring from *him*? The Council gave it to him."

But the answer came at once: "And the Council gave him companions, so that the errand should not fail. And you are the last of all the Company. The errand must not fail." (2:341)

Sam takes the Ring, and at once he feels its heaviness, but he is also growing in strength so that he can carry it. Shortly after, he perceives a flock of orcs and he puts on the Ring to hide. This sharpens his senses, and he can hear what the orcs are talking about.

But Sam now feels the temptation of the Ring. This description may be the most precise for a psychological understanding of what the Ring is doing:

> Wild fantasies arose in his mind; and he saw Samwise the Strong, Hero of the Age, striding with a flaming sword across the darkened land, and armies flocking to his call . . . .
>
> In that hour of trial it was the love of his master that helped most to hold him firm; but also deep down in him lived still unconquered his plain hobbit-sense: he knew in the core of his heart that he was not large enough to bear such a burden . . . .
>
> "And anyway all these notions are only a trick," he said to himself. "He'd [Sauron] spot me and cow me, before I could so much as shout out. . . . Well, all I can say is: things look as hopeless as a frost in spring. Just when being invisible would be really useful, I can't use the Ring! . . . So, what's to be done?"

He was not really in any doubt. He knew that
he must go down to the gate and not linger any
more. (3:177)

This description makes it clear that the issue is what Jungians call inflation, a false grandiosity of the ego. The ability of the different characters to resist the Ring is directly related to their ability to put their own egos aside for something greater than themselves—that is, their narcissistic maturity. The more powerful the individual and therefore more able to wield the Ring according to his or her wishes, the more dangerous it is and the deeper they would be corrupted. But again, the wise know this and will not touch the Ring. Tolkien does not paint his characters as pure good—they could all fall if not for their conscious self-knowledge. Sam is capable of looking through his own grandiose fantasies, keeping his task clear before his eyes, and even maintaining hope.

He liberates Frodo, and he gives him back the Ring voluntarily. Sam is the only Ring-bearer who ever accomplishes this, apart from Tom Bombadil, who was immune to its power. Strangely, on Sam the Ring seems to have only the long-ranging effect that he becomes stronger and grows in personal integrity. Even in the Land of Shadows, Sam has a vision of something higher, a white star over a mountaintop:

The beauty of it smote his heart, as he looked up
out of the forsaken land, and hope returned to him.
For like a shaft, clear and cold, the thought pierced
him that in the end the Shadow was only a small and
passing thing: there was light and high beauty for ever

beyond its reach. His song in the Tower had been defiance rather than hope; for then he was thinking of himself. Now, for a moment, his own fate, and even his master's, ceased to trouble him. He crawled back into the brambles and laid himself by Frodo's side, and putting away all fear he cast himself into a deep untroubled sleep. (3:199)

From the information in the *Silmarillion*, one must assume that the star is Eärendil's ship carrying the Silmaril. Eärendil, the half-elf, was the only mortal who ever reached the shores of Valinor. His errand, on behalf of both elves and men, was to implore the Valar to take action against the predecessor of Sauron, Morgoth—which they did. Ever after, Eärendil sails on the sky as a star to bring hope to men and elves.

Sam's consciousness has become vastly expanded. Now he understands that his duty is not only to his master but has a higher source. On the last part of the road in Mordor, Sam faces the danger without fear. He knows he must destroy the Ring and die with his master. But just as he gives up the hope of personal survival, a strange thing happens in that he grows in strength. On the Mount Doom, he carries Frodo, who carries the Ring (3:217–18).

There Sam has his final confrontation with Gollum, who attacks him and again separates him from his master. Frodo walks away while Sam is preparing to kill Gollum. But Gollum does not defend himself; he cries and says that when the Ring is gone, he will die in any case, so he asks Sam please to let him live.

But deep in his [Sam's] heart there was something
that restrained him: he could not strike this thing
lying in the dust, forlorn, ruinous, utterly wretched.
He himself, though only for a little while, had
borne the Ring, and now dimly he guessed the
agony of Gollum's shriveled mind and body,
enslaved to that Ring, unable to find peace or
relief ever in life again. (3:222)

Sam lets Gollum go and forgets all about him in looking for
Frodo, and the treacherous Gollum knocks Sam unconscious
and jumps on the invisible Frodo to bite off the finger with
the Ring. On the psychological level, it is impossible to think
that Sam could have consciously overruled his master and
destroyed the Ring himself. Here, we may understand Gollum
to be functioning as Sam's shadow in the service of the self.

While the volcano belches forth fire, Sam keeps a
clear head and saves them both. Of his original childlike
enthusiasm, he still has an indomitable optimism combined
with an unselfish overview, as when he sees Frodo and
himself as a part of a much greater story (which is, of course,
The Lord of the Rings):

"All the big important plans are not for my sort.
Still, I wonder if we shall ever be put into songs or
tales. We're in one, of course; but I mean: put into
words, you know, told by the fireside, or read out
of a great big book with red and black letters, years
and years afterwards. And people will say: 'Let's
hear about Frodo and the Ring!' And they'll say:
'Yes, that's one of my favourite stories. Frodo

was very brave, wasn't he, dad?' 'Yes, my boy,
the famousest of the hobbits, and that's saying
a lot.'" (2:321)

This makes Frodo laugh and feel lighter at heart:

"But you've left out one of the chief characters:
Samwise, the stouthearted. 'I want to hear more
about Sam, dad. Why didn't they put in more
of his talk, dad? That's what I like, it makes me
laugh. And Frodo wouldn't have got far without
Sam, would he, dad?'" "Now, Mr Frodo," said
Sam, "you shouldn't make fun. I was serious."
      "So was I," said Frodo. (2:322)

Frodo has every reason to think so. Unlike Frodo, Sam
plays an important role in the restoration of the Shire
(see page 197), and he becomes the mayor for many years.
Instead of being a single hobbit's servant, he will serve
all the hobbits in the Shire. Psychologically, the feeling
function becomes the integrating function in the renewal
of consciousness.

Merry and Pippin

In Elrond's council, Frodo's two young nephews insist on
joining the Company as though they were just going out on
an exciting adventure:

"We don't want to be left behind. We want to go with
Frodo."

"That is because you do not understand and cannot imagine what lies ahead," said Elrond.

"Neither does Frodo," said Gandalf, unexpectedly supporting Pippin. "Nor do any of us see clearly. It is true that if these hobbits understood the danger, they would not dare to go. But they would still wish to go, or wish that they dared, and be shamed and unhappy. I think, Elrond, that in this matter it would be well to trust rather to their friendship than to great wisdom." (1:289)

In traditional cultures, there are certain rituals to be undergone wherein young boys are turned into warriors, called rites of passage by anthropologists. Dangerous archetypal forces are activated in such transformational periods and so a crisis is at hand. The first stage is to acknowledge the beginning of the crisis—the youngsters have deviated from their usual course, and now they must be exiled from the community. In the second stage, they are isolated and often put to painful tests. They are taught the tribal lore and they are initiated. Finally, in the third stage, they are reintegrated into the community with a new social status. All of this can be viewed as a symbolic death and rebirth to a new life.

In the case of Pippin and Merry, there is of course no prearranged ritual, but their fate on the journey and back home to the Shire follows the archetypal pattern.

Pippin is the one who sets violent infernal powers in motion when he drops a stone into a deep well in Moria's mines and thereby alarms the orcs and arouses the Balrog.

Gandalf scolds him as one would a child, and even though Gandalf seemingly dies in the resulting fight, nobody ever blames Pippin in the least. He is simply regarded as not being responsible yet. Merry and Pippin play only a very small part in the journey until the critical moment arrives for the Company at the river Rauros.

The stage of separation begins brutally, when the young hobbits are carried off by the orcs. During the long run to the borders of Fangorn, they have to endure pain and physical hardship. We experience the journey through the eyes of Pippin from the time he wakes up after being unconscious, that is, the part of the ego that Pippin represents is becoming conscious. Now his impulsive, curious, and bright mind comes to the fore; the function of intuition is put to work. Pippin is a Took, and the Tooks were for many generations Thains in the Shire. A Thain was a kind of general over the hobbit army and the closest the hobbits came to having a chief. The Took family was special beyond that; it was both rich and numerous and had tended in every generation to bring forth great personalities with strong characters and adventurous temperaments (1:18–19).

Pippin quickly takes his chances to cut the rope around his hands when a dead orc lands on him. Later on in the run, he sees in his inner vision the face of Aragorn tracking them, and he sees how the small hobbit tracks are hidden by the tracks of the big heavy orcs. Impulsively, he breaks out of line to set his tracks separately, and he even has enough presence of mind to drop his elven bracelet on the ground. "'There I suppose it will lie until the end of time,' he thought.

'I don't know why I did it. If the others have escaped, they've probably all gone with Frodo'" (2:53).

Later, the orcs are attacked by the riders of Rohan, and before the hobbits can flee, they are taken by their necks by a big orc, who gropes them. Again, Pippin's intuition immediately grasps the meaning of the situation: "Grishnákh knows about the Ring! He's looking for it, while Uglúk is busy: he probably wants it for himself" (2:58). Although Pippin is very afraid, he begins to play up to the desire of the orc with hints. Soon Merry understands his aim and helps. The orc runs away with them in the direction of Fangorn, and he is killed by a rider, who doesn't notice the two small hobbits in their grey elven cloaks.

Merry and Pippin flee into Fangorn, where Merry takes the lead. He spent the time in Rivendell studying maps, therefore he has a good sense of where they are. Despite the warnings they had against Fangorn, Merry is not afraid of the forest; at home, he was accustomed to the Old Forest. The change of focus is typical of the difference between Pippin and Merry: where Pippin is an intuitive, Merry is a sensation type who notices the concrete details about everything. Merry's full name is Meriadoc, meaning "the protector from the sea." Merry's family, the Brandybucks, are actually the only hobbits who don't fear the sea and are happy sailing on rivers.

The initiation of boys into warriors includes a stay in "another world," an underworld or a symbolic womb that replaces the boy's tie to his real mother. The ancient forest serves well as an image for such a world. Here Merry and Pippin meet Treebeard, oldest of all living beings (older than or contemporary with the elves) (Tolkien 1999, p. 41). From a psychological point of view, special trees are often a symbol of the Self.

As warriors-to-be, Merry and Pippin find a formidable mentor and general in Treebeard. He teaches them ancient lore and causes them actually to grow several inches by feeding them ent-drinks. On the other hand, their presence initiates the action of Treebeard. His army of ents and huorns conquer Saruman and his enormous host of uruk-hai, and Isengard is destroyed. Merry and Pippin are witnesses to this battle without being in the battle themselves. But they are being prepared for the warrior role.

In the third stage of the rites of passage, the young men are integrated into the group of grownup warriors. In *The Lord of the Rings*, this happens when King Théoden, in company with Gandalf, Legolas, Aragorn, and Gimli, finds Merry and Pippin in the ruins of Isengard, peacefully smoking and sleeping. For the first time in the story, the hobbits are recognized as a race:

> "So these are the lost ones of your company, Gandalf?
> The days are fated to be filled with marvels. Already
> I have seen many since I left my house; and now here
> before my eyes stand yet another of the folk of legend.
> Are not these the Halflings, that some among us call
> the Holbytlan?"
>
> "Hobbits, if you please, lord," said Pippin.
>
> "Hobbits?" said Théoden. "Your tongue is
> strangely changed; but the name sounds not unfitting
> so. Hobbits! No report that I have heard does justice
> to the truth." (2:163)

Once again, Pippin's curiosity is the determining factor in the events. He cannot resist gazing into the palantir that Wormtongue threw from Orthanc, and through it the Eye sees him. As a result, Gandalf brings him to Minas Tirith while Merry stays with King Théoden of Rohan and becomes his sword-thain on March the 6th. Pippin offers his sword to Steward Denethor on March the 9th.

Now both Pippin and Merry have become soldiers. Merry is soon performing a great deed: in the battle outside Minas Tirith, when the Nazgûl captain fights with Éowyn over the dead king's body, Merry finds his courage and cuts the sinew behind the Nazgûl's knee so that he stumbles forward. Éowyn chops off his head, and the undead being dissolves like smoke. Pippin's achievement takes place simultaneously inside the city, and it is of another kind. Through his resolution, he saves Faramir from death when the mad Denethor commits suicide. Pippin also fights in the last battle and is wounded there.

When the two friends finally meet again, Merry still recovering on his sickbed, Pippin says:

"We Tooks and Brandybucks, we can't live long on
the heights" [that is, in the company of such highborn
people as Gandalf and Aragorn].
   "No," said Merry, "I can't. Not yet, at any rate. But
at least, Pippin, we can now see them, and honour
them. It is best to love first what you are fitted to love,
I suppose: you must start somewhere and have some
roots, and the soil of the Shire is deep. Still there
are things deeper and higher; and not a gaffer could
tend his garden in what he calls peace but for them,

whether he knows about them or not. I am glad that I know about them, a little. But I don't know why I am talking like this. Where is that leaf? And get my pipe out of my pack, if it isn't broken." (3:146–47)

The two young hobbits have really matured—and grown in a literal way. To Sam, the most amazing thing after the reunion of the four hobbits is Merry's and Pippin's height: "Can't understand it at your age! . . . But there it is: you're three inches taller than you ought to be, or I'm a dwarf" (3:234). Together with Sam, the young warriors will play a decisive part in the renewal of the Shire (see page 195).

3   THE JOURNEY OUT: ARCHETYPES OF TRANSFORMATION

Words like *crossroad, milestone, ford, border, ascent, descent, entrance,* and *exit* are still used in the symbolic sense as well as in the literal sense. They have not been emptied of inner meaning. This points back to a time when crossing a ford or a border or choosing a direction at a crossroad really were not just physical events but also spiritual transitions that demanded religious attention and rituals. For example, in ancient Greece, statues of Hermes stood by crossroads, as he was the god of travelers and might help to choose the right way. In a time before maps and GPS devices and in unknown lands there was no way to know what to expect after you crossed the ford or the border—unless you had a guide, human or spiritual.

These situations are archetypal. They are loaded with psychic energy even though they are not personified. The members of the Fellowship of the Ring were not only transformed via the foes and friends they met on the journey; they were also changed by the journey itself.

The Landscapes: Rivers and Forests

Just as most hobbits fear the sea, they also view rivers and boats with the greatest suspicion. The exception are the Brandybucks who live between the Shire proper and the Old Forest. Frodo's father was married to a Brandybuck, and when Frodo was a kid, his parents went sailing on the Brandy River. Nobody knows what really happened, but it is a fact that they drowned and left Frodo an orphan.

The motif of crossing a river appears in a fateful way four times in *The Lord of the Rings*. Every time, the crossing marks a choice of destiny.

The first river crossed is the Brandywine. Frodo feels heavy of heart, both because he is followed by the Black Riders and because he believes he soon has to be separated from his three friends. The dense fog symbolizes the emotional climate, too. For Sam, this is the first time in his life that he has crossed any river, and his thoughts characterize the situation well: "his old life lay behind in the mists, dark adventure lay in front" (1:109).

When Frodo is approaching the second river, the Bruinen which forms the border to Rivendell, he is seriously wounded and the fog is inside his mind. Everything around him is fading to ghostlike grey shadows. The danger is intensified; all nine Black Riders are coming together at the ford to overcome Frodo. He is, however, riding the white elf-horse belonging to Glorfindel, and he crosses the river in the nick of time. The Black Riders follow into the water and Frodo, in his borderline condition from the far shore, is able to see white spirit horses rise in the waves of the river, and behind the Black Riders on the opposite shore he sees Glorfindel in all his glory. Then he faints (1:227).

A wholly other situation exists when the Company is about to cross the third river, the Celebrant (or Silverlode), the border of Lórien, the mysterious Golden Wood that only Aragorn really knows. To cross the Celebrant is dangerous in a psychological way: in the Golden Wood one will meet oneself. Guided by the elf Haldir, the Company crosses the strong stream by means of three slender ropes (1:361). They are blindfolded before they can go on, and they are told that they will not get out alive unless the queen allows it.

The fourth river is the Anduin, which divides west from east and the free world from Sauron's dark world. Across Brandywine a civilized ferry sailed; to cross the Bruinen there was a ford and regular traffic; and crossing the Celebrant was accomplished on a temporary bridge set up by an expert. But the western bank of the Anduin has no connection to the other side.

The crossing of the rivers is a symbolic expression for a change in the conscious attitude and the result of a decision. By the Anduin at the falls of Rauros the final decision has to be made by Frodo. As Sam says, while the Company is waiting:

"Now it's come to the point, he's just plain terrified. That's what his trouble is. Of course he's had a bit of schooling, so to speak—we all have—since we left home, or he'd be so terrified he'd just fling the Ring in the River and bolt." (1:419–20)

When Frodo and Sam cross the Anduin, it is a point of no return. It is a journey into the kingdom of shadows, most likely into death.

Just as the hobbits cross four rivers, they also travel through four forests: the Old Forest, the troll forest, the Golden Wood (Lothlórien), and Fangorn. All the forests are clad in rumors of danger and neither hobbits nor dwarfs nor men set foot in them gladly. However, the forests were not always isolated enclaves. At one time, one could walk all over Middle-earth through the forests and the different beings had contact with each other. Now strangers are looked upon with suspicion.

Psychologically, the forests represent energetic centers in the collective unconscious. The risk of being overwhelmed by the unconscious is shown in symbolic ways, as when the hobbits lose their way, fall asleep, and are eaten by trees as happens in the Old Forest. But the forests also reveal a positive aspect of the unconscious as a source of help and inspiration, far beyond the hobbits' own powers. One can understand the forests and their rulers as parts of a fragmented Self. The four aspects of the Self are connected by the journey, because of its importance for all involved.

I shall interpret Tom Bombadil and Galadriel in later chapters from another angle, but here I will discuss how these two, together with Glorfindel and Treebeard, constitute hidden resources in the forest world of Middle-earth.

Merry unlocks the gate that forms the border between the Shire and the Old Forest, and the hobbits walk through it and into the forest—leaving their known world. "'There!' said Merry. 'You have left the Shire, and are now outside, and on the edge of the Old Forest'" (1:121). In the Old Forest, the trees are alive and some of them are mean. The Old Willowman eats Merry and Pippin and sings Frodo to sleep. As they make their way toward Bombadil's house, it gets dark, and the hobbits hear mysterious sounds and see strangely twisted faces everywhere: "They began to feel that all this country was unreal, and that they were stumbling through an ominous dream that led to no awakening" (1:132).

But in the middle of the forest is Bombadil's house and no evil can get in there. The dreamlike character about the landscape marks it . . . well, as dreamlike! The whole journey from the moment the hobbits leave the Shire until they return can be seen as one big dream.

Tom and Goldberry represent a paired image of the Self, a *syzygy*, close to nature and the ancient origins of creation:

> the hobbits sat half in wonder and half in laughter:
> so fair was the grace of Goldberry and so merry and
> odd the caperings of Tom. Yet in some fashion they
> seemed to weave a single dance, neither hindering the
> other, in and out of the room, and round about the
> table; and with great speed food and vessels and lights
> were set in order. (1:143)

From Tom the hobbits begin to learn how to protect themselves. First, Tom teaches the hobbits a magic song to call him to them. Such a simple calling spell is often told in fairy tales so that the hero can call his magic helper, whether it be a person or an animal. During the journey, both Frodo and Sam eventually use more sophisticated songs stemming from elven lore as a kind of magic prayer to Varda, the goddess of Middle-earth. Second, Tom equips the three younger hobbits with ancient weapons for protection.

While the Old Forest is close to the Shire, the troll forest is close to Rivendell (1:220). There are no trolls anymore, although we do meet the three stone trolls who originally appeared in *The Hobbit*. Bilbo and the dwarves were about to be eaten by the trolls, but Gandalf fooled them by keeping them talking until dawn. Trolls are turned into stone by sunlight. In *The Hobbit*, there were no good powers in this forest. But in *The Lord of the Rings*, the troll forest reveals a strong magical helper. The travelers meet the elf-warrior Glorfindel, who is looking for them. He lends his white horse to the wounded Frodo so that he can cross the ford. Even without his horse, Glorfindel reaches the ford almost as quickly as Frodo, who sees him there in his other, spiritual shape. Glorfindel is a strange figure who disappears from the story after a few lines in the discussion at Elrond's Council. Whereas the figure of Bombadil points backward in history and into the eco-matrix of nature, Glorfindel represents a dynamic, spiritual aspect of the Self.

The Golden Wood lies in the center of Middle-earth. It is strongly defended by magic as well as by elf-warriors and fearful rumors. At the heart of the forest is Queen Galadriel's tree-town, Caras Galadon (1:368). It is the feminine counterpart to the masculine Minas Tirith in Gondor—the tree people versus the stone people.

The city is described as a mandala: a large circular area is enclosed by a moat, and inside the moat is a green rampart around a lush green hill grown with tower-tall golden *mallorn* trees. In the foliage shine countless lamps with green, gold, and silver lights. After a long ascent, the Company reaches a glittering fountain in front of the mightiest of all the trees. In the uppermost crown of the tree is Galadriel's and Celeborn's gold-roofed house.

This is the seat of wisdom in Middle-earth, and the place of self-knowledge. Again, the Self is personified as a syzygy. But this time, it is a much more differentiated image and the feminine part is in the foreground. Both Goldberry and Galadriel are associated with the element of water, but where Goldberry is a kind of water nymph, Galadriel is a sublime spiritual figure. She knows about what was, what is, and what will come.

The fourth forest is Fangorn, neighboring Saruman's Isengard. Like the other forests, it is rumored dangerous. But Merry and Pippin soon meet Treebeard, the oldest of the tree shepherds, the Ents. The Ents are very special creatures who came into existence in the time of Creation, because the Vala Yavanna wanted a guardian for the trees, as dwarves, elves, and men would cut them down and use them for their own purposes (1999, p. 46). The Ents do not have towns, but they get together at the Entmoot on a special grass-clad area encircled by a high dark evergreen hedge (2:82). In the middle stand three silver birches and three paths lead to the area. While we still have a mandala here, it has a tripartite structure instead of being divided by four, which is unusual in *The Lord of the Rings*, where the number four pops up again and again. This expresses an unbalanced condition among the Ents; the Entwives disappeared long ago, so there is no feminine component.

Treebeard is an overwhelming figure, a highly original creature made out of Tolkien's fantasy, and yet strangely familiar. He, too, is a Self symbol, referring to the connection of the human psyche with the biosphere. In common with Tom Bombadil, Treebeard is also called "the oldest." As the first of his species, Treebeard is, according to alchemical philosophy, an "original man," an Anthropos—"the first man and the first tree and the first created of everything whatsoever" (Jung 1942, par. 168, note 64).

As the Entwives have gone there are no more entlings, but Merry and Pippin are sort of adopted and fed with a drink that makes them grow. In the same way Treebeard wakes up to revolt against Saruman because of what the hobbits tell him, Merry and Pippin later become leaders in the revolt against the tyrants who have infested the Shire.

Descent: Death and Rebirth

Although the crossings of the rivers are connected with fateful decisions and the entrances into the forests are surrounded by ominous rumors, these amount to little compared with the terror surrounding the descent. Darkness, evil, ghosts, and death are to be expected there, and it is only due to dire necessity that the subterranean roads are chosen.

When the hobbits are bewitched by the Barrow-wight and are lying in the grave, it is through no choice of their own; they have simply lost their way. The death and rebirth motif, however, is unmistakable. What the hobbits take away from this experience is the growing recognition that the quest may cost them their lives.

The importance of death in Tolkien's work (as in human psychology) cannot be overestimated. Death becomes a reality during the long walk through the darkness in the mines of Moria. It is dangerous for the whole Company, and they have to battle orcs and other monsters. But what they believe to be the death of Gandalf is the worst.

Frodo and Sam go through their entire part of the journey believing that Gandalf has died. Gandalf's own story about his descent to the underworld with the Balrog—his death and rebirth—he tells to Aragorn, Legolas, and Gimli when they meet in Fangorn. This is also the first time that the reader gets a glimpse into Gandalf's true nature:

> "Long I fell, and he fell with me. His fire was about me. I was burned. Then we plunged into the deep water and all was dark. Cold it was as the tide of death: almost it froze my heart."
>
> "Deep is the abyss that is spanned by Durin's Bridge, and none has measured it," said Gimli.
>
> "Yet it has a bottom, beyond light and knowledge," said Gandalf. "Thither I came at last, to the uttermost foundations of stone. He was with me still. His fire was quenched, but now he was a thing of slime, stronger than a strangling snake.
>
> "We fought far under the living earth, where time is not counted. Ever he clutched me, and ever I hewed him, till at last he fled into dark tunnels. . . . Far, far below the deepest delvings of the Dwarves, the world

is gnawed by nameless things. Even Sauron knows them not. They are older than he." (2:105)

From the underworld, the pair ascends again, up the endless stairs to fight on the summit of Durin's Tower. The battle on the summit is taking place in their spirit shapes; those watching would only see that a storm is raging over the mountaintop, and they would hear thunder and see lightning. The Balrog is finally crushed against the mountainside and the tower falls. Gandalf dies, but he is returned to life, naked upon the mountain.

This is a wholly symbolic battle with the classical four elements—a descent in fire and heat; then water and cold; then earth, stone, and slime; and an ascent to the final battle in the air, again involving the other elements: fire as lightning, water as ice and rain, and the rock itself as "the hard horn of the world" (2:106).

The Balrog is a Maia, a spirit like Gandalf. The Maiar were the servants of the Valar, and the Balrogs served the fallen Vala Melkor in the oldest times. Sauron himself was originally the servant of Melkor. The burning underworld is suggestive of the image of hell in the Middle Ages. The fight is between below and above, the vertical direction pointing to the spiritual aspect of this event. As Gandalf dies and reappears, his savior role is more than hinted at.

Three times, Aragorn receives messages about the Paths of the Dead. The first one, from Galadriel, sounds ominous:

> But dark is the path appointed for thee:
> The Dead watch the road that leads to the Sea. (2:106)

Next, Elrohir, the son of Elrond, brings the message from his father with these words: "*The days are short. If thou art in haste, remember the Paths of the Dead*" (3:48). Still, Aragorn hesitates until his relative, Halbarad, brings the message from Arwen: "*The days now are short. Either our hope cometh, or all hopes end. Therefore I send thee what I have made for thee. Fare well, Elfstone!*" (3:48).

This is finally the fateful time for Aragorn and Arwen. Elrond had also reminded Aragorn of the words of the seer who said that Isildur's heir would take the Paths of the Dead and call the ghosts to battle. Aragorn now sees that this is his only choice.

The journey along the underground path is pictured through the terrified mind of Gimli:

> he was ever hindmost, pursued by a groping horror
> that seemed always just about to seize him; and a
> rumour came after him like the shadow-sound of
> many feet. He stumbled on until he was crawling like
> a beast on the ground and felt that he could endure
> no more: he must either find an ending and escape or
> run back in madness to meet the following fear. (3:61)

Well out of the underground and heading toward the Stone of Erech, the army of ghosts evokes terror wherever it comes:

> Lights went out in house and hamlet as they
> came, and doors were shut, and folk that were afield
> cried in terror and ran wild like hunted deer. Ever
> there rose the same cry in the gathering night: "The

King of the Dead! The King of the Dead is come
upon us!" (3:62)

The old fear of the dead broods densely around the Hill of
Erech with its stone at the top. It is a tall black stone, formed
like a ball; maybe it fell from the sky. By this stone, Aragorn
has the dead swear loyalty; the army of ghosts rides east for
five days and nights, and all foes flee. As Gimli later tells
it: "Strange and wonderful I thought it that the designs of
Mordor should be overthrown by such wraiths of fear and
darkness. With its own weapons was it worsted!" (3:152).

Just as superhuman as Gandalf's vertical fight with the
Balrog seems to be the horizontal achievement of Aragorn.
It is basically a psychic force he reveals; this battle is spiritual,
too. The weapon is fear, not sword. At variance with the
mythological wild ride of Wotan, this is a process of purifying
the land of thousand-year-old ghosts, and of foes, too. In the
process, Aragorn proves himself to be the true heir of Isildur.

The wandering of Frodo and Sam in Mordor takes place
between the 26th of February and the 25th of March and
is a very different kind of descent than that of Gandalf and
Aragorn. No superhuman or magic force is at work—slowly
the hobbits walk in circles; frequently off track, they suffer
from hunger and thirst and spiritual pains. In Mordor,
everything is about darkness, death, and destruction. As
Tolkien writes in the foreword:

> One has indeed personally to come under the shadow
> of war to feel fully its oppression; but as the years go
> by it seems now often forgotten that to be caught in
> youth by 1914 was no less hideous an experience than

to be involved in 1939 and the following years. By 1918 all but one of my close friends were dead. (1:7)

World War I put its psychological stamp on Tolkien. Just as Jung, during this war, was drawing his first mandala to keep himself in balance, Tolkien was creating his first drafts of invented languages and mythology in the soldier's canteens, in overfilled huts, in tents by candlelight, even in trenches under fire. But he transferred the terrors of war to an archetypal level. In the online paper, "J. R. R. Tolkien and World War I," Nancy Marie Ott describes how Tolkien's sublimated war experiences come through:

> The parallels between the landscapes of No-Man's Land and Tolkien's landscapes of nightmare are striking. Mordor is a dry, gasping land pocked by pits that are very much like shell craters. Sam Gamgee and Frodo Baggins even hide in one of these pits when escaping from an Orc band, much as a soldier might have hidden in a shell hole while trying to evade an enemy patrol. Like No-Man's Land, Mordor is empty of all life except the soldiers of the Enemy. Almost nothing grows there or lives there. The natural world has been almost annihilated by Sauron's power, much as modern weaponry almost annihilated the natural world on the Western Front. (2002)

The ghastly landscapes with the horrible stench near Mordor are compared with descriptions of how it was to be in the trenches with mutilated and rotting corpses of men and animals everywhere. Tolkien was at the frontier, but he was not physically wounded. He contracted so-called trench fever in October 1916 and spent the next half a year in a hospital.

It is most likely that Tolkien's illness was what is today called posttraumatic stress disorder (PTSD). But at that time, many officers still regarded this psychic suffering as cowardly.

Even though the descriptions of Frodo's sufferings spring from the author's firsthand experience with PTSD, they are—like everything else with a possible personal background—elevated to the archetypal dimension and characterized as a result of a too close intercourse with evil. Tolkien knows a lot about the faces of evil and the conditions determining its origins and growth.

Frodo and Sam enter Mordor March 12th to 15th. There are actually three entrances: the first after they both come through the lair of Shelob; the second when Sam passes the gate with the silent watchers alone to save Frodo, and the third and final entrance when both Frodo and Sam overcome the watchers. And then they struggle along on the endless wandering in the dry land toward the Fire Mountain, or Mount Doom as it most often was called.

> Far away now rising towards the South the sun,
> piercing the smokes and haze, burned ominous, a
> dull bleared disc of red; but all Mordor lay about the
> Mountain like a dead land, silent, shadow-folded,
> waiting for some dreadful stroke. (3:222)

Inside the mountain is the Crack of Doom:

> the heart of the realm of Sauron and the forges of
> his ancient might, greatest in Middle-earth; . . . all at

once there came a flash of red . . . now leaping up, now
dying down into darkness; and all the while far below
there was a rumour and a trouble as of great engines
throbbing and labouring. (3:222)

Again we are reminded of an image of hell from the
Middle Ages. Indeed, hell breaks loose in the shape of the
uncontrolled activity of the volcano when Sauron falls.
Frodo and Sam expect death "here at the end of all things,"
but already unconscious, "the wanderers were lifted up and
borne far away out of the darkness and the fire" (3:229).

The Changing of the Wind

For days, the sun was invisible because of the darkness
spreading from Mordor. However, on March 15th a natural
phenomenon occurs: the wind changes and drives the
darkness away. This is noticed by all the main characters
from their different positions, and they all interpret it as a
spiritual event.

We first hear of it when the Nazgûl captain, already well
inside the broken gate of Gondor, threatens Gandalf with
death. But in that moment a cock crows saluting a new dawn
after several days of eternal night. As though in answer,
Rohan's great horns blow wildly (3:103).

In the next chapter, we are taken back into the previous
night with Théoden, accompanied by the king of the Púkel
men, who had guided the troops on a fast and swift road to
Minas Tirith; in this case, the darkness of Mordor was actually helpful in covering their movements. Just as Ghân-buri-

Ghân is taking leave with Théoden, a light comes into his eyes: "'Wind is changing!' he cried, and with that, in a twinkling as it seemed, he and his fellows had vanished" (3:109).

Aragorn arrives with his ships,

> borne upon a wind from the Sea to the kingdom of Gondor . . . . But the hosts of Mordor were seized with bewilderment, and a great wizardry it seemed to them that their own ships should be filled with their foes; and a black dread fell on them, knowing that the tides of fate had turned against them and their doom was at hand. (3:123)

Later, Legolas and Gimli tell Merry and Pippin how they experienced the sailing. After the ships were conquered, they worked hard on the oars but moved forward slowly because they rowed against the stream. Suddenly Legolas laughs:

> "'Up with your beard, Durin's son!' he said. 'For thus is it spoken: *Oft hope is born, when all is forlorn.*' . . .
> ". . . at midnight hope was indeed born anew. Sea-crafty men of the Ethir gazing southward spoke of a change coming with a fresh wind from the Sea. Long ere day the masted ships hoisted sail, and our speed grew, until dawn whitened the foam at our prows." (3:153)

Simultaneously, in Mordor, Frodo and Sam have escaped the orcs and have begun the last walk toward Mount Doom. For a time they hide below a cliff because they feel a Ringwraith circling high over them. Then it disappears. Frodo gets up:

and then they both stared in wonder. Away to their left, southward, against a sky that was turning grey, the peaks and high ridges of the great range began to appear dark and black, visible shapes. Light was growing behind them. Slowly it crept towards the North. There was battle far above in the high spaces of the air. The billowing clouds of Mordor were being driven back, their edges tattering as a wind out of the living world came up and swept the fumes and smokes towards the dark land of their home. Under the lifting skirts of the dreary canopy dim light leaked into Mordor like pale morning through the grimed window of a prison.

"Look at it, Mr Frodo!" said Sam. "Look at it! The wind's changed. Something's happening. He's not having it all his own way. His darkness is breaking up out in the world there. I wish I could see what is going on!" . . . .

As Frodo and Sam stood and gazed, the rim of light spread all along the line of the Ephel Dûath, and then they saw a shape, moving at a great speed out of the West . . . . As it went it sent out a long shrill cry, the voice of a Nazgûl; but this cry no longer held any terror for them: it was a cry of woe and dismay, ill tidings for the Dark Tower. The Lord of the Ringwraiths had met his doom. (3:196)

As a reader, one feels strongly with the main characters that the changing of the wind is a good omen and brings hope to everybody, even though everything looks worse than ever.

Works of Men: The Towers

The night before Frodo leaves the Shire, he dreams about the sound of the sea. He is on a dark heath looking up on a tall, white tower standing on a high ridge. He begins to climb the ridge with the intention of ascending the tower to see the sea. But suddenly lightning is glistering over the sky, followed by a thunderclap (1:119).

The white tower in Frodo's dream is the tallest of the three immensely ancient elf towers west of the Shire. From this tower, one can see the sea, say the hobbits, even though none of them had ever climbed it: "the Sea became a word of fear among them, and a token of death, and they turned their faces away from the hills in the west" (1:16). Frodo's fascination with the sea later appears associated with death—but at the same time the western sea route of the elves also represents the mortal's longing for transcendence.

These are the only towers built by elves that we hear about. But a great number of other towers appear in *The Lord of the Rings*, and most are ill-fated places. Evil is generated from Barad-dûr and springs like electric sparks from tower to tower: Don Goldur, Orthanc, Mordor's watchtowers, Minas Ithil (Morgul), the watchtower Cirith Ungols. On the maps of Middle-earth one can see many more anonymous towers.

Apart from the western elf towers and the eastern Barad-dûr, these towers are the work of men—as opposed to the other elements in the landscapes: rivers, forests, and wind. The towers are connected to historical events. In Tolkien's descriptions, they are associated with teeth and eyes and crowns—the towers are like heads looking far away, ruling and biting. They can be said to symbolize the knowledge and power in the collective consciousness. The decay of the towers reveals how this consciousness has become dull and corrupt over the centuries (see also chapter 8, "The Old King").

The positive collective consciousness personified in the legendary kings of old used the palantir in the towers to keep Gondor and Arnor together. The palantir were elvish inventions. Although more refined than a modern broadband and a web camera, they worked a bit like that. For a long time, it was believed that all the stones were lost. But as it turns out, Sauron was able to work his evil influence on both Orthanc and Minas Tirith by means of the remaining palantir.

The first tower that the hobbits meet on their quest is Weathertop, or Amon Sûl, a thousand-year-old ruin that originally was part of the defenses of the northern kingdom against the Witch-king in Angmar (1:197). On Weathertop, Aragorn tells how Elendil once stood there looking for Gil-galad at the end of the Second Age, before the battle where Sauron was conquered and lost his Ring. And he also tells them about Beren, a man, and the elf princess Lúthien and how they finally were united after many trials and tribulations. Beren and Lúthien are, of course, the mirror of Aragorn himself and Arwen.

The hobbits are becoming part of the great history of the world. Weathertop, however, is a place of defeat, and Frodo is almost destroyed when the Nazgûl attack. Their king is identical to the Witch-king from Angmar, who lives on as an undead Ring spirit, a Ringwraith.

Isengard is Saruman's stronghold. Its tower, Orthanc, was originally built for observing the stars. While the other towers were meant for defense and as communication centers across the lands of Middle-earth, Orthanc watched upward to the sky. It was structured as a mandala: a huge low bowl in a natural ring wall of tall cliffs with a tower five hundred feet tall built in the midst. It was constructed of four mighty pillars joined into one but separated again to form four horns near the summit. This is associated with evil; in certain alchemical texts, the Devil was described as a four-horned snake trying in vain to lift its horns into the heavens (Jung 1955–56, par. 494).

The circle formed on the plain was once green and filled with avenues and orchards. But now everything is barren and filled with pillars, chains, and deep shafts to subterranean caves. "Iron wheels revolved there endlessly, and hammers thudded. At night plumes of vapour steamed from the vents, lit from beneath with red light, or blue, or venomous green" (2:160).

Orthanc has become the incarnation of the ongoing demonic pollution and destruction of living nature, and it is deeply satisfactory to the reader when the forest, stirred to action by Treebeard, begins to move. Merry and Pippin have arrived at the high western ridge:

> At last they stood upon the summit and looked
> down into a dark pit: the great cleft at the end of the
> mountains: Nan Curunír, the Valley of Saruman.
> "Night lies over Isengard," said Treebeard. (2:90)

Indeed, against the Ents Saruman has no defense. After Aragorn becomes king, he entrusts Orthanc to the Ent's custody.

The moon tower, Minas Ithil, situated at the western border of Mordor, is silver white and at the top it has a moon stone. Once it was beautiful, but it has been completely overtaken by Sauron and renamed Minas Morgul. It is a spooky place, surrounded by a wavering light like an exhalation of decay, a corpse light. The windows in the tower are like countless black holes looking inward into emptiness. A white bridge passes over the stream and a road winds up to the city gate. On every side are shadowy meads with pale flowers:

> Luminous these were too, beautiful and yet horrible
> of shape, like the demented forms in an uneasy
> dream; and they gave forth a faint sickening charnel-
> smell; an odour of rottenness filled the air. (2:313)

Frodo is suddenly gripped by a trance and runs forward while his head is lolling from side to side. The Ring drags him, and he is threatened by madness. The moon tower in its decay symbolizes a psychotic condition.

The other tower on Mordor's western side is Cirith Ungol's tower, a stronghold originally built by the old kings to keep their enemies inside Mordor. Its gate is open, but the way is barred by the silent Watchers, two stone statues, each with three heads with vulture faces. Visible or invisible, none can pass unheeded (3:178).

The Watchers form a mental barrier that Sam breaks with courage, will—and Galadriel's light, which the Watchers fear. When Sam and Frodo together cross the gate for a second time, Sam cries out to the Vala queen, Varda, and Frodo continues in elvish language with a sentence meaning "Hail you, brightest Star!" "The will of the Watchers was broken with a suddenness like the snapping of a cord, and Frodo and Sam stumbled forward. . . . the wall above crumbled, and fell in ruin" (3:192). Their cries had worked like a magic prayer that was heard on the highest place.

Minas Tirith in Gondor has the last free tower. The city was founded as the center of Middle-earth, with seven circular levels, one above the other, and seven gates through which the road winds upward to the high castle. There the river springs at the foot of the White Tower. Originally its name was Minas Anor, the sun tower, and the great city gate was directed east toward the rising sun. Behind the gate was a bastion of stone formed like a ship's keel facing east. This bastion reached to the upper circle. It was built confronting the moon tower with the star city Osgiliath situated at the Anduin River between the two towers.

Minas Ithil has been transformed into Minas Morgul, and even in Minas Tirith decay has begun. The long-missed king, the decreasing population, and the withered white tree all speak to its decline. The ruling steward, Denethor, is well into his corruption by Sauron through the seer stone and his own greed.

4 THE TRICKSTER

The Old Forest with its master, Tom Bombadil, forms the border area between the Shire and the wide world—or, psychologically, between the smaller world of consciousness and the bigger world of the collective unconscious. As a border figure, Tom is an image of the archetypal trickster: "Trickster appears on the border of or just beyond the existing boundaries, classifications and categories" (Hynes and Doty 1993, p. 34). In many tribal cultures, ritual clowns appear at the cult drama, just before the great gods enter the scene; we still know the trickster as the clown from the circus who delights children and simple souls.

To Frodo's question about who Tom is, Goldberry answers:

> "He is," said Goldberry. . . ."He is, as you have seen
> him. . . . He is the Master of wood, water, and hill."
> "Then all this strange land belongs to him?"
> "No indeed! . . . That would indeed be a burden
> . . . . The trees and the grasses and all things growing
> or living in the land belong each to themselves. Tom
> Bombadil is the Master. No one has ever caught
> old Tom walking in the forest, wading in the water,
> leaping on the hill-tops under light and shadow. He
> has no fear. Tom Bombadil is master." (1:135)

Later, Frodo asks Tom if he heard him call for help at the river or if it was just coincidence that brought him to the hobbits. Tom's answer is, to say the least, not clear and simple:

> "Eh, what?" he said. "Did I hear you calling? Nay, I did not hear: I was busy singing. Just chance brought me then, if chance you call it. It was no plan of mine, though I was waiting for you. We heard news of you, and learned that you were wandering. We guessed you'd come ere long down to the water: all paths lead that way, down to Withywindle. Old grey Willow-man, he's a mighty singer; and it's hard for little folk to escape his cunning mazes. But Tom had an errand there, that he dared not hinder." (1:137)

Tom sings a song about himself collecting water lilies for Goldberry, which was very lucky for the hobbits as this only happens once a year. Tom's nature seems to be such that he trusts completely in the principle of the creative moment or the meaningful coincidence, which Jung termed synchronicity.

Once again Frodo asks Tom who he is. This comes after Tom has been singing to the hobbits of ages so ancient that they sit enchanted before him under a sky filled with white starlight. Tom says:

> "Don't you know my name yet? That's the only answer. Tell me, who are you, alone, yourself and nameless? But you are young and I am old. Eldest, that's what I am. Mark my words, my friends:
> Tom was here before the river and the trees; Tom remembers the first raindrop and the first acorn. He

made paths before the Big People, and saw the little People arriving. . . . When the Elves passed westward, Tom was here already, before the seas were bent. He knew the dark under the stars when it was fearless— before the Dark Lord [Melkor] came from Outside." (1:142)

When Elrond later hears this story in the Council, he says that he had forgotten Bombadil and that maybe he should have asked him to join the meeting. "Iarwain Ben-adar we called him, oldest and fatherless. . . . He is a strange creature" (1:278). Gandalf, however, doesn't think that Tom would have wanted to come and neither does he believe it to be a good idea to ask him to guard the Ring, even if it holds no power over him.

> "He is his own master. But he cannot alter the Ring itself, nor break its power over others. And now he is withdrawn into a little land, within bounds that he has set, though none can see them, waiting perhaps for a change of days, and he will not step beyond them." (1:279)

Glorfindel and Galdor both believe that if everything else were conquered, Bombadil would also fall, the last one just as he was the first, and then night would come. Galdor adds that Bombadil has no power to put against the enemy unless such power exists in earth itself (1:279).

From all these remarks, it is obvious that the elves just don't know very much about Tom Bombadil beyond his name—the oldest and the fatherless—which hints toward his spirit nature. Even Gandalf, although himself a spirit, a

Maia, does not know Tom Bombadil very well.

When the war is over, Gandalf intends to go and talk properly with Tom:

> "He is a moss-gatherer, and I have been a stone
> doomed to rolling. But my rolling days are ending,
> and now we shall have much to say to one another."
> (3:275)

But what they will talk about and who Tom is, the reader is never told. In a letter, Tolkien writes that Tom Bombadil is an enigma on purpose. Tolkien, who otherwise explains all and everything in the *Silmarillion* and in the appendices to *The Lord of the Rings,* does not explain Tom.

Perhaps the enigma is related to Tom's presence close to the Shire. His knowledge about the hobbits easily matches that of Gandalf.

> He appeared already to know much about them and
> all their families, and indeed to know much of all
> the history and doings of the Shire down from days
> hardly remembered among the hobbits themselves.
> It no longer surprised them; but he made no secret
> that he owed his recent knowledge largely to Farmer
> Maggot. (1:143)

The first evening Tom easily pulls the true story of the real errand of the hobbits out of Frodo. "Show me the precious Ring!" he suddenly says in the middle of his story, and to his own amazement Frodo pulls it off its chain and passes it over to Tom (1:144).

An amazement it certainly is for the reader, too, as we already know how extremely difficult it is to let go of the Ring. Tom puts it up to his eye—as though he wants to show a joyous blue counterpart to Sauron's terrifying evil eye. Then he puts the Ring on his finger—without becoming invisible. He throws it up in the air and makes it disappear before he gives it back to Frodo with a smile. The Ring obviously doesn't hold any power over Tom, who alone of all beings can treat it like a plaything. Frodo suddenly becomes suspicious; maybe Tom has exchanged the Ring with another? He puts it on for the first time—and he does become invisible to his friends, but not to Tom, who calls Frodo back to order as though he were a somewhat troublesome child:

> "Your hand's more fair without it. Come back! Leave
> your game and sit down beside me! We must talk
> a while more, and think about the morning. Tom
> must teach the right road, and keep your feet from
> wandering." (1:144)

Although Tom himself is immune to magic, he teaches the hobbits a magic rhyme to use if they ever need him. This rhyme is put to good use by Frodo against the Barrow-wight.

Tom's extremely long memory, when compared with the mythology in Tolkien's *Silmarillion*, implied that his origins go back to the time of the creation of the world. He has to be either a Vala or a lesser spirit, one of the companions of the Valar.

According to the creation myth, there was a first battle between Melkor and the other Valar, and Melkor withdrew for a time (Tolkien 1999, p. 11). The Valar descended to the earth and took on the form and shape of the elves and men, which they had seen in the vision of the One. They collected many companions, and the earth was for a time a beautiful garden without disruption (ibid., p. 21). So there was a paradisial age, although we are not informed of its length. After this age, Melkor returned and took on a visible form. Tom says about himself that he "knew the dark under the stars when it was fearless—before the Dark Lord [Melkor] came from Outside" (1:142).

Tom Bombadil in the Old Forest, like the Valar, is able to sing the power out of evil and make others feel safe. Tom could also be a spirit of another special kind. His exact nature is not so important for the psychological interpretation of the story; what is certain and central is that Tom is outside the question of power and evil and does not really fit any known category.

The word *trickster* refers literally to one who does tricks, and the typical trickster lies, cheats, swindles, and, in general, treats norms and boundaries with great impudence. This is not what Tom does at all, but he is playful and impossible to define. The Trickster crosses boundaries, he does what you just don't do, says forbidden things; nothing is too holy, no norms exist that will not be broken. The Trickster turns the world upside down by pulling things into the light that are hidden in the dark. One very important pattern in the Trickster is that he crosses a forbidden line to bring light to humankind.

From this point of view, it makes sense that Tom pulls the Ring out of its hiding place and makes fun with it, when everybody else takes it with deadly seriousness. At a time when the entire world has reason to worry deeply, Tom is singing and dancing and jumping about—completely carefree. Apart from keeping Goldberry happy and "my making and my singing, my talking and my walking, and my watching of the country" (1:156), Tom desires nothing; he has no goals, no plans. In his world, things are happening by themselves. He likes to find out about things and beings, but he does not do anything about them. Accordingly, he has no need to remove the evil things from his own kingdom; they just don't get in his way.

Even Tom's ancient age and close relationship to nature, which have led many to interpret him as a nature spirit, is typical for the Trickster. Jung claims that the Trickster mirrors an ancient psychic structure, an undifferentiated consciousness, close to the animal kingdom. Many Trickster figures are animals, such as the Native American Coyote or the Hindu monkey god, Hanuman. The Trickster is simultaneously completely unconscious and has superhuman qualities. Most mythological Tricksters have a malicious, primitive aspect that is foreign to Tom. But in Middle-earth at this time, there is a rich supply of evil beings; Tom personifies the benign aspect instead.

The Trickster may appear in a person's personality when he or she is in a stressed situation or going through a time of conflict. This is, of course, the case for the hobbits who are between two different worlds and who need help to cross the line between the homely world and the great unknown in front of them.

Jung writes about the Trickster archetype:

> It is a personification of traits of character which
> are sometimes worse and sometimes better than
> those the ego-personality possesses. A collective
> personification like the trickster is the product of
> an aggregate of individuals and is welcomed by each
> individual as something known to him, which would
> not be the case if it were just an individual outgrowth.
> (1954b, par. 468)

In this sense, Tom's special interest in hobbits may be significant. They have much in common: their cheerfulness and happiness, their strong inclinations toward good, plentiful meals and the use of strong colors in their clothes; even their rootedness. Tom Bombadil could be seen as a kind of local hobbit god who protected or hid them simply through his presence. He is totally immune to the lure of the Ring, but even the hobbits seem to have qualities that make them resist the Ring in a way other beings cannot.

5   THE HERO

The universal hero myth is always about

> a powerful man or god-man who vanquishes evil in
> the form of dragons, serpents, monsters, demons, and
> so on, and who liberates his people from destruction
> and death. The narration or ritual repetition of sacred
> texts and ceremonies, and the worship of such a figure
> with dances, music, hymns, prayers, and sacrifices,
> grip the audience with numinous emotions (as if
> with magic spells) and exalt the individual to an
> identification with the hero. (Jung 1972, p. 79)

In mythologies from around the world, figures of heroes
have many traits in common regardless of their origins. These
traits also appear in the dreams and fantasies of modern
times. What do they mean on the psychological level? As
a rule of thumb, one can say that they appear when the ego
needs support for a task it cannot master without help from
the resources contained in the unconscious. Henderson
points out that there are various aspects of the archetypal
hero depending on the development of the ego and the age
and maturity of the individual (cited in Jung 1972, p. 127ff).
But on all levels, the image of the hero has a relation to the
group and in a wider sense to the cultural group.

For almost a thousand years, no kings ruled in Gondor; a lineage of stewards ruled in the king's stead. Arnor, the northern kingdom of old was destroyed by the Witch-king, the same person who we meet in *The Lord of the Rings* as the captain of the Ringwraiths. The son of the last king took the title of chief of the Dúnedain, and all the heirlooms of the northern kingdom were given into the care of Elrond in Rivendell. From that time on, the descendants of the king, the heirs of Isildur, were secretly brought up by Elrond until Aragorn's time. Aragorn appears as the archetypal cultural hero, whose task is to found a kingdom for a new age and reunite the kingdoms of Arnor and Gondor.

Another feature of the archetype is that the hero grows up in hiding and does not know his true identity. Aragorn's lineage could hardly be nobler among men. He descends from the great kings of Númenor, a group of islands where men, in the Second Age, lived in a golden age until the wildly grandiose king Ar-Pharazôn attacked Valinor itself with the intention of winning immortality for men. Then Númenor perished in a great flood. But Elendil stayed loyal toward the Valar; he survived the catastrophe and founded an exiled kingdom—Middle-earth—with his sons, Isildur and Anárion.

Aragorn lost his father early in his life, and he lived in Elrond's house with his mother under the name Estel (hope). When Aragorn was twenty years old, Elrond revealed to him his true name and lineage and gave him the sword that was broken and the ring of Barahir. About the time Aragorn was told of his ancestors, he met Arwen for the first time and fell in love with her. A relationship of love between a mortal man and an immortal elf princess was already present in the history of Aragorn's kin as well as in Arwen's on her mother's side. Aragorn is a descendant of Beren and Lúthien, who lived in the oldest times.

Beren and Lúthien were the original model for a loving couple in Tolkien's fantasy; he even had these names inscribed on the gravestone for himself and his wife. When the orphaned Tolkien, sixteen years old, was living in a boarding house, he fell in love with Edith, who was three years older. His foster father, a priest, forbade him to see her for several years, but when World War I broke out, Tolkien proposed to her by letter and married her. Then he volunteered for the army, fell ill, and returned home with posttraumatic stress disorder and his self-invented cure—the elf languages and escapism, which transformed his beloved into an elf princess and his own sufferings into heroic deeds on a grand scale. This is another example of how Tolkien was able to elevate a core of personal experience to an archetypal level.

In the *Silmarillion*, Lúthien's father demanded that Beren obtain the Silmaril from the crown of Melkor before he can have Lúthien. This was an impossible task, and it succeeded only through Lúthien's active support. Beren was mortally wounded, but by the intervention of the Valar, he was brought back to a life together with Lúthien. Lúthien had to sacrifice her immortality, just like Arwen eventually does for Aragorn.

Aragorn's mother saw what was happening to her son, and she was afraid that Aragorn had aimed too high and that he would risk losing the friendship of Elrond. Elrond, however, did not become angry. He called Aragorn to his side and foretold of the great destiny ahead of him. Either he would rise above all his forefathers since Elendil or fall into the darkness. In all the years of his trials, he must not take a wife.

The waiting time was to be sixty-two years. Aragorn met Gandalf and served a kind of apprenticeship with him:

> Thus he became at last the most hardy of living Men, skilled in their crafts and lore, and was yet more than they; for he was elven-wise, and there was a light in his eyes that when they were kindled few could endure. His face was sad and stern because of the doom that was laid on him, and yet hope dwelt ever in the depths of his heart, from which mirth would arise at times like a spring from the rock. (3:341)

Aragorn continued to travel on his dangerous journeys over most of Middle-earth, more often than not in the service of Gandalf, but known only as a wanderer, one of the so-called Travelers.

Strider is the name Aragorn goes by when the hobbits first meet him. They are uncomfortable with his rascally looks, to say the least, and especially with the fact that he seems to know about their errand. He bears with them for some time, but then he cuts the discussion of his intentions short:

> "If I was after the Ring, I could have it—NOW!"
> He stood up, and seemed suddenly to grow taller. In his eyes gleamed a light, keen and commanding. Throwing back his cloak, he laid his hand on the hilt of a sword that had hung concealed by his side. They

did not dare to move. Sam sat wide-mouthed staring at him dumbly.

"But I *am* the real Strider, fortunately," he said, looking down at them with his face softened by a sudden smile. "I am Aragorn son of Arathorn; and if by life or death I can save you, I will." (1:183)

Aragorn demonstrates his integrity by being above temptation; as Isildur's heir, he knows too well that the Ring was Isildur's Bane. More than anybody, he is friend and confidant of Gandalf; he thinks it fair enough that Isildur's heir must repair Isildur's wrongdoing. In the absence of Gandalf, Aragorn takes on the role of guide and guardianship of the hobbits. In dreams, this is still a typical function of the hero archetype; such figures may come forth to support a still weak and childish ego.

In Rivendell, when Elrond gives a lecture in the history of the Third Age and each of the newly gathered characters submits his piece of the puzzle, it becomes obvious that the fateful time for Aragorn is approaching. Boromir, son of the Gondor steward, tells a dream that both he and his brother had:

"the eastern sky grew dark and there was a growing thunder, but in the West a pale light lingered, and out of it I heard a voice, remote but clear, crying:

Seek for the Sword that was broken:
In Imladris it dwells;
There shall be counsels taken
Stronger than Morgul-spells.
There shall be shown a token

> That Doom is near at hand,
>> For Isildur's Bane shall waken,
>>> And the Halfling forth shall stand." (1:259)

The dream, of course, is prophetic. All the signs are present. Aragorn now reveals his heirloom, the sword that was broken. Frodo, the Halfling, shows the Ring, Isildur's Bane. When Elrond appoints the Company, Aragorn is an obvious member.

> "I would have begged you to come," said Frodo, "only I thought you were going to Minas Tirith with Boromir."
> "I am," said Aragorn. "And the Sword-that-was-Broken shall be re-forged ere I set out to war. But your road and our road lie together for many hundreds of miles. Therefore Boromir will also be in the Company. He is a valiant man." (1:289)

But Boromir is of the opinion that the Ring should be wielded as a weapon. Only hesitantly, he accepts the decision of those wiser:

> "Then in Gondor we must trust to such weapons as we have. And at the least, while the Wise ones guard this Ring, we will fight on. Mayhap the Sword-that-was-Broken may still stem the tide—if the hand that wields it has inherited not an heirloom only, but the sinews of the Kings of Men." (1:281)

This remark foreshadows the potential conflict between Aragorn and Boromir, as the latter is not happy about Aragorn's implicit demand for the throne of Gondor. But valiant he is, and he is still unconscious of his desire to have the Ring of Power for himself.

Aragorn's sword is forged anew, and he gives it a new name: Andúril, Flame of the West. It is engraved with strong runes and an emblem—seven stars between the crescent moon and a sun surrounded by rays. The forged sword is an obvious symbol of Aragorn's masculine strength.

When the Company is gathering to leave Rivendell, Aragorn sits with his head bowed to his knees. Only Elrond really knows that Aragorn now begins his heroic quest with the superhuman task of winning the crowns of both Gondor and Arnor—his reward being the elf princess Arwen as his bride. Aragorn's real goal has nothing to do with the Ring or power; his motivation and goal is love. This makes him incorruptible.

After the apparent death of Gandalf, Aragorn takes the Company to Lórien, where he is very welcome. There is no doubt that he is a favorite of the queen. Almost forty years have passed since he came to Lórien for the first time, and even then Galadriel saw something in him that neither his own mother nor Elrond could fathom. She herself dressed him in silver and white, with a grey elven cloak, and put a radiant gem on his brow—and looking like that, she let her granddaughter Arwen meet him under the golden trees. It was then that Arwen made her choice and promised to become a mortal for his sake. Elrond accepted this, but he said that his daughter should not shorten her life for anybody less that the king of both Gondor and Arnor: "To me then even our victory can bring only sorrow and parting—but to you hope of joy for a while" (3:342).

When the Company takes its leave, Galadriel asks if Aragorn has a wish for a present of departure. Aragorn says:

"Lady, you know all my desire, and long held in keeping the only treasure that I seek. Yet it is not yours to give me, even if you would; and only through darkness shall I come to it." (1:391)

The treasure he is thinking of is, of course, Arwen, and Galadriel cannot give him this. However, she can give him a special gift from Arwen, an heirloom from Galadriel herself: a silver brooch in the shape of an eagle with outspread wings as a setting for a clear green gem—a token of hope and a bidding to take his kingly name: Elessar, Elfstone of Elendil's House. In the eyes of his friends, Aragorn changes in an almost physical way: they had not before noticed how tall he is and how kingly his countenance.

While Arwen is, throughout the story, the faraway and motivating goal although she is hardly ever present, Galadriel is indeed an active presence. To Aragorn, she appears as a spiritual mother, just as Gandalf has become his spiritual father. The two most powerful figures in the whole story work together to complete Aragorn's destiny—which fits into their own, as both have the goal of crushing Sauron's power. Mythological heroes often have powerful, magic, or divine helpers and allies; this too is a feature of the archetype.

When Frodo, at the falls of Rauros, has to decide his further course, Aragorn also has a difficult decision to make. Originally he thought that Boromir's dream was a plain message for him to go to Minas Tirith and fight for Gondor. But now with Gandalf missing he knows that he can no longer leave the Ring-bearer if Frodo chooses to enter Mordor. The shadow conflict with Boromir is also lurking; Boromir speaks softly, as though to himself, and lapses without the otherwise keen Aragorn taking notice:

> "But if you wish to destroy the armed might of the
> Dark Lord, then it is folly to go without force into
> his domain; and folly to throw away." He paused
> suddenly, as if he had become aware that he was
> speaking his thoughts aloud. "It would be folly to
> throw lives away, I mean," he ended. (1:385)

Amon Lhaw and Amon Hen are the cliffs where the high seats of hearing and of sight stood at the time of the great kings. Boromir follows Frodo to the summit and his violent desire for the Ring induces him to try to take it by force. However, when Frodo has disappeared, Boromir trips over a stone and comes back to his senses: "'What have I done? Frodo, Frodo!' he called. 'Come back! A madness took me, but it has passed. Come back!'" (1:416).

Frodo is not coming back, and confusion splits the Company. Boromir is mortally wounded while he is defending Merry and Pippin against a host of orcs. Aragorn finds him dying, and Boromir confesses his evil deed to him, saying that he has failed.

> "No," said Aragorn, taking his hand and kissing his
> brow. "You have conquered. Few have gained such a
> victory. Be at peace! Minas Tirith shall not fall!" (2:16)

This is another example of a shadow figure resolving a conflict of duty; just like Gollum resolved Sam's potential conflict, Boromir's action actually simplifies Aragorn's choice. Finally, he clearly feels that the destiny of the Ring-bearer has been lifted out of his hands, and that his duty is to save Merry and Pippin from the orcs.

Aragorn, Legolas, and Gimli track the orcs in an incredible race across the plains of Rohan where they run into Éomer, nephew of King Théoden. Aragorn reveals himself by drawing Andúril:

> "Elendil!" he cried. "I am Aragorn son of Arathorn, and am called Elessar, the Elfstone, Dúnadan, the heir of Isildur Elendil's son of Gondor. Here is the Sword that was Broken and is forged again! Will you aid me or thwart me? Choose swiftly!"
>
> Gimli and Legolas looked at their companion in amazement, for they had not seen him in this mood before. He seemed to have grown in stature while Éomer had shrunk; and in his living face they caught a brief vision of the power and majesty of the kings of stone. For a moment it seemed to the eyes of Legolas that a white flame flickered on the brows of Aragorn like a shining crown. (2:36)

It is the first time that Aragorn openly declares his claim to the throne of Gondor and it transfigures him. Éomer sees it, and he unconditionally recognizes Aragorn as Gondor's true king. In contrast to his orders, he not only lets Aragorn and his friends pass, he also lends them horses to ride on.

In Fangorn they run into the arms of Gandalf, who has

come back from the dead. Gandalf gives Aragorn a message from Galadriel, but only after the victorious fight at Helm's Deep does it become clear what the message means. That is the point at which they are found by the relatives of Aragorn, the Dúnedain, the Grey Company, together with Elrond's sons, Elladan and Elrohir. Elrohir brings Aragorn another message, from Elrond: *"The days are short. If thou art in haste, remember the Paths of the Dead"* (3:48).

His kinsman, Halbarad, gives Aragorn a tall staff—a furled standard—a gift made by Arwen, along with her message, by and large the same words for the third time: *"The days now are short. Either our hope cometh, or all hopes end. Therefore I send thee what I have made for thee. Fare well, Elfstone!"* (3:48).

Now the days are short! With this decisive push from his beloved, Aragorn now really steps into his role. He has challenged Sauron by showing himself in his kingly shape in the Orthanc palantir (3:53), and he needs to reach Minas Tirith in time. Only one road is possible: the Paths of the Dead. The old seer predicted that when Isildur's heir summoned the host of the dead at the Stone of Erech, they would have to obey and fight Sauron to fulfill the oath to Isildur they once broke.

To the final ordeal of the archetypal hero belongs "the night journey," a journey through the underworld, where from the hero ascends like the rising sun. The subterranean ride corresponds to this motif, and it is the rebirth motif that transforms Aragorn into a king.

The army of the dead follows Aragorn through the Morthond valley:

95

Lights went out in house and hamlet as they came,
and doors were shut, and folk that were afield cried in
terror and ran wild like hunted deer. Ever there rose
the same cry in the gathering night: "The King of the
Dead! The King of the Dead is come upon us!" (3:62)

And then they reached the black stone of Erech where the
dead promise to fulfill their oath. Terrified, the enemies
drown or flee before them. Legolas later remembers:

"In that hour I looked on Aragorn and thought how
great and terrible a Lord he might have become in the
strength of his will, had he taken the Ring to himself.
Not for naught does Mordor fear him. But nobler is
his spirit than the understanding of Sauron; for is he
not of the children of Lúthien? Never shall that line
fail, though the years may lengthen beyond count."
(3:152)

Aragorn captures a fleet from the enemy and sails on the
river to Minas Tirith. From his ship the wind now displays
the standard Arwen gave him: on a black field flowers the
white tree symbolizing Gondor. But the seven stars and
the high crown above the tree are the signs of Elendil, his
ancestor. Arwen made the stars out of gems and the crown
out of mithril and gold.

Despite the victory, Aragorn hesitates to enter the city
because of a possible conflict with its ruler, Lord Denethor.
What Aragorn doesn't know is that the steward has burned
himself to death and that his younger son, Faramir, is mortally
wounded, as are Éowyn and Merry. An old woman who helps

the healers sighs over their condition and expresses the wish that there were still a king in Gondor: "For it is said in old lore: *The hands of the king are the hands of a healer.* And so the rightful king could ever be known" (3:136). Gandalf takes her point and sends for Aragorn, who arrives incognito. By means of the herb kingsfoil, Aragorn calls Faramir back from the shadow of death:

> Suddenly Faramir stirred, and he opened his eyes, and he looked on Aragorn who bent over him; and a light of knowledge and love was kindled in his eyes, and he spoke softly. "My lord, you called me. I come. What does the king command?"
>
> "Walk no more in the shadows, but awake!" said Aragorn. "You are weary. Rest a while, and take food, and be ready when I return."
>
> "I will, lord," said Faramir, "For who would lie idle when the king has returned?" (3:142)

Faramir recognized Aragorn as his king although he has never seen him before. Faramir is depicted as an ideal moral figure; although he met Frodo and Sam and guessed his brother Boromir's temptation and tragic fate, Faramir himself was not tempted by the Ring: *"Not if I found it on the highway would I take it,* I said" (2:289). Accordingly, Faramir also yields gracefully to Aragorn, whereas Boromir, not to speak of old Denethor, probably not would have given up power that easily.

The rumor that the king has returned spreads like a fire through the city. The sick and wounded come to him, and

Aragorn is helped by Elrond's sons, who are also healers. To-gether they work through the night. People notice Aragorn's silver brooch with the green gem, and they spontaneously call him Elfstone because of this. Thus his own people give him the name it was foretold he should take (3:147). What is unusual about Aragorn as a hero figure—that he is primary motivated by love—also shows in this healing sequence. Before he takes on his role of ruler, he wins the hearts of his people.

After the fall of Sauron, Frodo and Sam meet again with the transformed Aragorn in Ithilien on the Field of Cormallen. In an opening in a flowering forest at the river, three high seats have been built of green turfs. To the right is the standard of Rohan, to the left the standard of Prince Imrahil, and in the middle the one with the white tree, the high Crown and the seven stars on a black field.

> On the throne sat a mail-clad man, a great sword was
> laid across his knees, but he wore no helm. As they
> drew near he rose. And then they knew him, changed
> as he was, so high and glad of face, kingly, lord of
> Men, dark-haired with eyes of grey. (3:232)

In April, Aragorn rides with his armies to the gates of Minas Tirith, and the citizens, with Faramir at the fore, are ready to receive Aragorn:

> He was clad in black mail girt with silver, and he wore
> a long mantle of pure white clasped at the throat with
> a great jewel of green that shone from afar; but his
> head was bare save for a star upon his forehead bound
> by a slender fillet of silver. (3:244)

So he arrives dressed in a way that symbolizes the union of opposites in the form of black and white, but his own color is green.

Faramir brings the old king's crown which belonged to Eärnur. The crown is formed like a tall white helm, and the wings on its sides are wrought with pearls and silver. Seven adamants are set in a small circlet with a single flaming jewel in the middle. Aragorn lifts up the crown and quotes the words of his ancestor, Elendil, when he first came over the sea from the west: "Out of the Great Sea to Middle-earth I am come. In this place will I abide, and my heirs, unto the ending of the world" (3:246). But Aragorn does not crown himself; he asks Frodo to bring the crown to him and asks Gandalf to put it on his head. This Gandalf does with the words: "Now come the days of the King, and may they be blessed while the thrones of the Valar endure!" (3:246).

This is one of the very few explicit ritual sayings in the story, partly a blessing, partly a naming of the powers of Valinor. Most other sayings in which Valinor and the Vala are hinted at are spoken in elven language and not translated into English by Tolkien. But of course, *The Lord of the Rings* is a deeply spiritual book. Everything has a deeper meaning, a mysterious denseness of significance that often has its background in mythological events outside the story itself; these are hinted at but frequently not explained, even over the course of the story. This is also implicit in the description of King Aragorn:

> Tall as the sea-kings of old, he stood above all that
> were near; ancient of days he seemed and yet in the

flower of manhood; and wisdom sat upon his brow, and strength and healing were in his hands, and a light was about him. (3:246)

Finally, the night comes when Gandalf brings Aragorn to a high, sacred place on the mountain where only the kings ever had access. Gandalf says that all of this is Aragorn's kingdom and that it will become the heart of an even greater kingdom. A new age has begun, the Age of Men. Still, Aragorn doubts his fate, for when will he see the sign that he will be the founder of a dynasty—the only way mortals can continue?

Gandalf asks him to turn around and look behind him, and there on a stony slope at the edge of the snow, a young sapling of Gondor's white tree has sprouted. Aragorn takes it and plants it in the place of the old dead tree, and it grows and blossoms. The white tree of Gondor grew from the seeds of the tree that Isildur brought over the deep sea, and that tree descended from the oldest tree in the world, Telperion, which lit the world with a silver light, and from the fruits of that tree the moon was shaped. So now Aragorn knows the sign has been given.

On midsummer evening, the elven lords finally arrive with the bride of Aragorn. Elrond surrenders the scepter of Annúminas, the token of kingship of the two realms, Arnor and Gondor (3:251). The scepter is not a simple heirloom, however valuable; it symbolizes that the kingship of Middle-earth passes from Elrond to Aragorn—from the old king to the young, from the elves to men.

The mythological hero normally comes from the east like the rising sun, but in *The Lord of the Rings* Valinor, the Island of the Valar, lies west and everything good comes from the west. So the setting sun is shining on Aragorn, and Arwen is called Evenstar, the evening star. The imagery shows that Aragorn is blessed by the Valar, but the underlying archetypal imagery points toward the ending and death. In the *Silmarillion*, the mortality of men is called "the Gift of Ilúvatar," and Aragorn accepts his death, even though he lives much longer than ordinary people.

Aragorn and Arwen rule for one hundred and twenty years, and then one day Aragorn says that he will die now, while he is still whole. To choose the moment of passing away is a special ability he has inherited from the kings of Númenor. His parting with Arwen is very sad indeed. She yearns to hold him back. Aragorn tells her that she has known that this moment would come ever since she gave him her promise:

> "But let us not be overthrown at the final test, who of
> old renounced the Shadow and the Ring. In sorrow
> we must go, but not in despair. Behold! We are not
> bound for ever to the circles of the world, and beyond
> them is more than memory. Farewell!" (3:344)

Tolkien's description of Aragorn's death is a statement about a fully realized life of which death is an integrated part: "they saw that the grace of his youth, and the valour of his manhood, and the wisdom and majesty of his age were blended together" (3:344).

6   THE ANIMA

According to Jung, men carry inside of themselves an image of woman, or the anima. The first step on the road to self-knowledge is often the confrontation with the shadow, but in addition to the shadow, the anima also appears in men. The first appearance of the anima in *The Lord of the Rings* is when Frodo meets Goldberry, the daughter of the river: "'Fair lady Goldberry!' said Frodo at last, feeling his heart moved with a joy that he did not understand" (1:134). Frodo is enchanted in a way that reminds him of fair elven voices, but

> the spell that was now laid upon him was different:
> less keen and lofty was the delight, but deeper and
> nearer to mortal heart; marvellous and yet not
> strange. (1:134)

In men's dreams and fantasies, the anima appears in many ways; in *The Lord of the Rings*, we meet just three versions. Goldberry is a type of anima figure that in fairy tales and myths appears as nymphs of rivers or forests. Arwen is another typical figure, the object of the romantic longings of Aragorn as well as his muse and inspiration. Galadriel, the third anima figure, is comparable to goddesses of wisdom, love, and war.

As the hobbits travel through Middle-earth, they meet the anima figures in gradually more differentiated and comprehensive forms. Arwen and Galadriel are not removed from nature, but compared with Goldberry they have a higher spiritual and historical insight.

As is typical of the nature anima, Goldberry represents the instinctual and sensual world. Tolkien rarely touches directly upon the subject of sex in *The Lord of the Rings*, but he does use a vocabulary of images that traditionally refer to sexuality when he describes Goldberry. In myth and fairy tales, the river nymphs and sea nymphs are often enchanting in a destructive way in that they lead the hero down the wrong track or even drown him. The hobbits' attempt to follow the river Withywindle by themselves would certainly have killed them if Tom had not been there.

In the poem "The Adventures of Tom Bombadil," which Tolkien wrote long before *The Lord of the Rings*, we see Tom following much the same route as the hobbits: he was eaten by the Old Willowman, he met the Barrow-wight, and he was drawn into the water by Goldberry (Tolkien 1975). But in contrast to the hobbits, Tom sent them all away with his song and walked unconquered back to his house. However, Tom couldn't forget Goldberry, and he walked back to the river and took her home as his bride with the words:

> "Here's my pretty maiden!
> You shall come home with me! The table is
>   all laden:
> yellow cream, honeycomb, white bread
>   and butter;
> roses at the window-sill and peeping round
>   the shutter.

You shall come under Hill! Never mind
   your mother
in her deep weedy pool: there you'll find no lover!"

(Tolkien 1989, p. 201)

The psychological point is that Goldberry's mother represents the dangerous and swallowing aspect of the feminine (like the monster spider Shelob). When mother and daughter are differentiated from one another, the daughter turns into a positive figure. It is obvious that Goldberry is happy and satisfied with her Tom. But the sexual word *lover* used in the earlier poem is not picked up again in *The Lord of the Rings*. Goldberry is described as an anima type close to the water and the flowers, lifted just above the unconscious element by Tom. She is his other half and does not seem to have a separate character of her own.

In Elrond's house, at the celebration of Frodo's healing, we are presented with a feminine figure of another order:

In the middle of the table, against the woven cloths
upon the wall, there was a chair under a canopy, and
there sat a lady fair to look upon, and so like was
she in form of womanhood to Elrond that Frodo
guessed that she was one of his close kindred. Young
she was and yet not so. The braids of her dark hair
were touched by no frost; her white arms and clear
face were flawless and smooth, and the light of stars
was in her bright eyes, grey as a cloudless night; yet
queenly she looked, and thought and knowledge were
in her glance, as of one who has known many things

that the years bring. Above her brow her head was
covered with a cap of silver lace netted with small
gems, glittering white; but her soft grey raiment had
no ornament save a girdle of leaves wrought in silver.
(1:239)

A much more dignified, spiritual figure is described here. Arwen, however, is also a typical anima figure in the sense that she never really becomes a person in her own right. We meet her only three times in *The Lord of the Rings*, that is, in Elrond's house, at the wedding with Aragorn, and finally when she symbolically renounces her immortality by passing her ticket to the elf ship on to Frodo.

In the appendices, Tolkien tells a little more of the love story of Arwen and Aragorn. It becomes clear that Arwen personifies Aragorn's inspiration and high goal. In this sense, she is to him what Beatrice was to Dante, a psychopomp.

Arwen leads to Galadriel in the direct connection wherein the last is the grandmother to the former and much, much older:

the hair of the Lady was of deep gold, . . . but no sign
of age was upon them, unless it were in the depths of
their eyes; for these were keen as lances in the starlight, and yet profound, the wells of deep memory.
(1:369)

She was herself of Noldo-kindred "and remembered the day before all days in Valinor, and she was the mightiest and the fairest of all the elves that still stayed in Middle-earth" (Tolkien 1999, p. 358). She was the last in Middle-earth among those who had led the Noldor into exile in

Beleriand; others of her kin had apologized to the Valar and were allowed back into Valinor, but Galadriel refused to apologize.

Lórien is geographically placed in the center of Middle-earth; it is the heart of elfdom on earth. Galadriel's realm is timeless, filled with golden trees, sunlight, and perfection. But Lórien is hidden from the ordinary world, and if anybody with evil intentions gets in, they will never get out alive. She knows "what was and is, and in part also what shall be" (1:372).

Although Celeborn is the lord, is it obvious that Galadriel is the ruling queen, the Lady of the Golden Wood. It was Galadriel who called the White Council together, although she did not have her wish to see Gandalf as its leader. She actively played the matchmaker between Arwen and Aragorn by dressing him up as an elf lord. Even before the Company leaves Lórien, Galadriel knows (but does not tell) that Gandalf is alive, and she commands the king of the eagles, Gwaihir, to carry Gandalf to Lórien, where she heals him. Also, she sends messages to the relatives of Aragorn, the Dúnedain, and to the two sons of Elrond to hasten to Aragorn's assistance.

Galadriel sees directly into the minds of the members of the Company.

> All of them, it seemed, had fared alike: each had felt
> that he was offered a choice between a shadow full
> of fear that lay ahead, and something that he greatly
> desired: clear before his mind it lay, and to get it he
> had only to turn aside from the road and leave the
> Quest and the war against Sauron to others. (1:373)

All of them had felt tested. Only Boromir thinks that Galadriel was tempting them but that he alone would not be tempted. He doesn't trust "this Elvish Lady," he says. But Aragorn answers that "there is in her and in this land no evil, unless a man bring it hither himself. Then let him beware!" (1:373).

Galadriel is a guide in the inner world and has forced all the members to look into themselves to detect if their loyalty is stronger than their personal wishes and desires. While Goldberry and Arwen are only experienced through the male projections, a differentiation has occurred when we meet Galadriel. She is clearly described as an object of projection for Boromir, as he misinterprets his own desire for the Ring and ascribes his doubtful motive to Galadriel. She is a complex character in her own right, as we can see in the scene where Frodo offers the Ring to Galadriel:

> "You are wise and fearless and fair, Lady Galadriel,"
> said Frodo. "I will give you the One ring, if you ask for
> it. It is too great a matter for me." (1:380–81)

Intuitively, Frodo has by this point tried to pass the Ring on to all three of the guardians of the great elf rings: first Gandalf, then Elrond, and now Galadriel. He hardly understands the extent of the temptation he puts before them, although Galadriel answers as though he were fully aware:

> Galadriel laughed with a sudden clear laugh.
> "Wise the Lady Galadriel may be," she said, "yet here
> she has met her match in courtesy. Gently are you

revenged for my testing of your heart at our first meeting. You begin to see with a keen eye. I do not deny that my heart has greatly desired to ask what you offer. For many long years I had pondered what I might do, should the Great Ring come into my hands, and behold! it was brought within my grasp. The evil that was devised long ago works on in many ways, whether Sauron himself stands or falls. Would not that have been a noble deed to set to the credit of his Ring, if I had taken it by force or fear from my guest?

"And now at last it comes. You will give me the Ring freely! In place of the Dark Lord you will set up a Queen. And I shall not be dark, but beautiful and terrible as the Morning and the Night! Fair as the Sea and the Sun and the Snow upon the Mountain! Dreadful as the Storm and the Lightning! Stronger than the foundations of the earth. All shall love me and despair!"

She lifted up her hand and from the ring that she wore there issued a great light that illumined her alone and left all else dark. She stood before Frodo seeming now tall beyond measurement, and beautiful beyond enduring, terrible and worshipful. Then she let her hand fall, and the light faded, and suddenly she laughed again, and lo! she was shrunken: a slender elf-woman, clad in simple white, whose gentle voice was soft and sad.

"I pass the test," she said. "I will diminish, and go into the West, and remain Galadriel." (1:381)

When Sam later describes Galadriel to Faramir, he says:

"Beautiful she is, sir! Lovely! Sometimes like a great tree in flower, sometimes like a white daffadowndilly, small and slender like. Hard as di'monds, soft as moonlight. Warm as sunlight, cold as frost in the stars. Proud and far-off as a snow-mountain, and as merry as any lass I ever saw with daisies in her hair in springtime." (2:288)

Galadriel's city is built by the living nature, as opposed to Elrond's house which is built of stone. Elrond's house associated with starshine and moonlight, while Lórien is associated with the sun. Galadriel's hair and her golden *mallorn* trees relate to Laurelin, one of the two trees that originally lit the world. Of the fruit of the Laurelin, the sun was created.

What we meet in Galadriel is an overwhelming goddesslike anima, an exalted figure of wisdom. The Catholic Tolkien may have been inspired by the notion of the Virgin Mary, but his imagination carries him far beyond the traditional version of Mary as the pure, humble, always merciful and loving servant. Galadriel is more akin to a figure of wisdom such as the Sophia in the Old Testament, who existed as the foster child and coworker of Yahweh even before the world was created, and she played on the wide earth and found joy in the children of men (Proverbs 8:22–31). She transmitted knowledge about the world and how the sun and the stars moved in the sky; she knew about medicine, plants, and all living beings, but also the course of history, signs, prophesies, and the thoughts of man (Wisdom 7:16–322, 8:8).

Seen from the perspective of male psychology, Galadriel is an anima figure who mediates between the archetype of the Self and consciousness. Mirrored in female psychology, she is a personification of the feminine self.

7 THE LOVE STORY: ÉOWYN AND FARAMIR

Among the all the couples in *The Lord of the Rings*, only one, Éowyn and Faramir, is formed between a man and a woman, and only their love story is told as a "real" one. The love between Aragorn and Arwen is the grand background of the story, of course, but the reader does not witness its development or the inner feelings of the two involved.

Superficially, Éowyn is modeled on the figure of a Viking shield-maiden such as they are described in the *Gesta Danorum* by Saxo Grammaticus: tall, proud women who dressed in arms like men and went into battle. On closer inspection, however, Tolkien has actually created a portrait of a conflicted modern woman who might well be called a feminist. She is the only feminine figure who resembles a real woman rather than an anima figure. She is the niece of Théoden, who loves her but has no eyes for her qualities. She stands behind the king's chair and waits upon him when the Company dines with him.

When the army is about to depart for the battle at Helm's Deep, Théoden declares her brother Éomer as his heir, if he should fall. But he needs somebody to rule the people that he leaves behind—who will do that? Nobody answers.

Théoden wonders whether there is really no one that they would trust. They trust in the House of Éorl, says Hama, but the king still doesn't get the message:

> "But Éomer I cannot spare, nor would he stay," said the king; "and he is the last of that House."
> "I said not Éomer," answered Háma. "And he is not the last. There is Éowyn, daughter of Éomund, his sister. She is fearless and high-hearted. All love her. Let her be as lord to the Eorlingas, while we are gone." (2:128)

The king accepts the advice, and Éowyn receives a sword and corselet.

After the victory at Helm's Deep, Aragorn rides quickly to Dysterharge and is received by Éowyn, who thinks he has come to see her. When Aragorn tells her that he only will spend the night and go on at dawn, she beams at him:

> "Then it was kindly done, lord, to ride so many miles out of your way to bring tidings to Éowyn, and to speak with her in her exile." (3:56)

She had already fallen in love with him when she first saw him, and now she falls silent and is deeply tormented when she understands that he will ride by the Paths of the Dead.

Later that night Éowyn calls to Aragorn in the darkness outside his lodge and tells him that if he must go that way she wants to ride with him to battle. He tells her that it is her duty to stay with her people and govern them until the king returns. Then her self-control breaks and what follows is a feminist broadside from Éowyn, which may seem somewhat unexpected from a writer as conservative as Tolkien:

> "All your words are but to say: you are a woman,
> and your part is in the house. But when the men
> have died in battle and honour, you have leave to
> be burned in the house, for the men will need it
> no more. But I am of the House of Eorl and not a
> serving-woman. I can ride and wield blade, and I
> do not fear either pain or death."
> "What do you fear, lady?" he asked.
> "A cage," she said. "To stay behind bars, until
> use and old age accept them, and all chance of
> doing great deeds is gone beyond recall or desire."
> (3:58)

The discussion that Éowyn puts up here has no origin in Saxo Grammaticus; it clearly belongs to the twentieth century. We find an identically expressed fear of cages in the heroine Athena in the short story "The Monkey," one of the *Seven Gothic Tales* (1934) by Karen Blixen. The maiden Athena also longs for battles and great deeds.

"Cage" is the negative version of the old word *bower*, meaning a shaded place (in this case for maids and ladies). In Old Danish, which Tolkien was able to read, the word *bur* would mean both things. Gandalf makes the connection clear when he speaks of Éowyn's sufferings before she was wounded by the Nazgûl:

> "But who knows what she spoke to the darkness,
> alone, in the bitter watches of the night, when all her
> life seemed shrinking, and the walls of her bower

closing in about her, a hutch to trammel some wild thing in?" (3:143)

Éowyn is also the only feminine being in *The Lord of the Rings* who is directly spoken of as an object of unwanted sexual desire—from Wormtongue—as well as welcome desire, later, from Faramir. Gandalf hints that Saruman has promised her as his reward:

> "What was the promised price? When all the men were dead, you were to pick your share of the treasure, and take the woman you desire? Too long have you watched her under your eyelids and haunted her steps." (2:124)

Éowyn stays with the people until the king returns, but when Théoden also forbids her to join the army that is going to Minas Tirith, she resolutely disguises herself as the soldier Dernhelm, and she hides Merry below her cloak. Her officer, Elfhelm, is probably aware of her true identity but lets her be.

In the big battle, when the king has been struck down by the Nazgûl captain and his winged dinosaur, Éowyn positions herself to defend Théoden's corpse from being eaten. . But the Nazgûl says: "Hinder me? Thou fool. No living man may hinder me!"(3:116). Then she laughs: "But no living man am I! You look upon a woman. Éowyn I am, Éomund's daughter" (3:116). For the first time, her womanhood comes to her advantage, and the Nazgûl is cut down. Although Éowyn is seriously wounded, her life is saved by Merry. She is brought to the Houses of Healing, and Aragorn discusses her condition with Éomer and Gandalf:

"When I first looked on her and perceived her unhappiness, it seemed to me that I saw a white flower standing straight and proud, shapely as a lily, and yet knew that it was hard, as if wrought by elf-wrights out of steel. Or was it, maybe, a frost that had turned its sap to ice, and so it stood, bitter-sweet, still fair to see, but stricken, soon to fall and die? Her malady begins far back before this day, does it not, Éomer?" (3:142–43)

Éomer thinks that she has fallen unhappily in love with Aragorn, but apart from that, he thinks that she was only filled with concern for the king in the days of Wormtongue. But the wise Gandalf makes it plain what Éowyn's problems were about:

"My friend," said Gandalf, "you had horses, and deeds of arms, and the free fields; but she, born in the body of a maid, had a spirit and courage at least the match of yours. Yet she was doomed to wait upon an old man, whom she loved as a father, and watch him falling into a mean dishonoured dotage; and her part seemed to her more ignoble than that of the staff he leaned on." (3:143)

Éowyn wakes up in despair. But also wounded is the handsome and tender Faramir, who is now the steward of Minas Tirith after the death of his father and brother. He, too, is a modern character, with the psychological problem that because he has great empathy and is interested in poetry and in the arts, his father does not think him a proper man—not like the more brutal and traditionally masculine older brother, Boromir. As Éowyn is an orphan, Faramir lost his beloved mother as a child. Neither of them really had understanding or appreciation from those persons from whom they most wanted it.

Éowyn asks to meet the steward; she hates to be confined in idleness, and she complains.

> He looked at her, and being a man whom pity deeply stirred, it seemed to him that her loveliness amid her grief would pierce his heart. And she looked at him and saw the grave tenderness in his eyes, and yet knew, for she was bred among men of war, that here was one whom no Rider of the Mark would outmatch in battle.
> "What do you wish?" he said again. "If it lies in my power, I will do it." (3:237)

For the first time, Éowyn doubts herself; she does not want Faramir to think she is childish, and so she ends up with a soft and sad complaint, that the healers want her to be confined in her chamber and she has no window toward the east.

Faramir answers that this he can do something about. She can walk in the garden in the sunshine and look east, as he does himself. It would ease his own care if she would join him. She wants to know why, as she does not want to speak to anybody. Faramir praises her beauty, and says:

> "For you and I have both passed under the wings of the Shadow, and the same hand drew us back."
> "Alas, not me, lord!" she said. "Shadow lies on me still. Look not to me for healing! I am a shieldmaiden and my hand is ungentle." (3:239)

Faramir is strongly attracted to Éowyn. He asks Merry about her, and he begins to understand her problems. The next morning, she stands on the walls, and from that day they walk or sit together, now in silence, now in speech. The healer sees with pleasure that they grow in strength each day. On the fifth day it is cold, and Faramir gives Éowyn a warm blue robe set with silver stars. It was made for his mother, and it always reminded him of his first loss, but now it becomes a symbol of how Faramir has transferred his love from mother to a woman of his own generation.

Together they wait until Fate strikes, and unconsciously they take each other's hands:

> Then presently it seemed to them that above
> the ridges of the distant mountains another vast
> mountain of darkness rose, towering up like a wave
> that should engulf the world, and about it lightnings
> flickered; and then a tremor ran through the earth,
> and they felt the walls of the City quiver. A sound
> like a sigh went up from all the lands about them; and
> their hearts beat suddenly again. (3:240)

The reader knows that the two are witnessing the fall of Sauron, but in this scene it is transformed into a symbol of an emotionally decisive event between them. The relation between Faramir and Éowyn has now intensified to love in a way that brings healing. The fall of evil in this situation symbolizes the dissolution of their trauma, although Éowyn is not yet conscious of it.

Golden days follow; swift riders bring tidings of the victory. Faramir is busy preparing the reception of the king.

Éowyn does not go to the Field of Cormallen, even though her brother asks her. Faramir goes to her and asks her whether it is because Aragorn himself did not ask her—or is it that she wants to stay with him for love?

> "I wished to be loved by another," she said. "But I desire no man's pity."
> "That I know," he said. "You desired to have the love of the Lord Aragorn. Because he was high and puissant, and you wished to have renown and glory and to be lifted far above the mean things that crawl on the earth. As a great captain may to a young soldier he seemed to you admirable. For so he is, a lord among men, the greatest that now is. But when he gave you only understanding and pity, then you desired to have nothing, unless a brave death in battle." (3:242)

Faramir's psychological understanding is precise; he goes on to tell her that he loves her and would now do so even if she was the happy queen of Gondor. Éowyn finally realizes that she loves him back.

> "I stand in Minas Anor, the Tower of the Sun," she said, "and behold! the Shadow has departed! I will be a shieldmaiden no longer, nor vie with the great Riders, nor take joy only in the songs of slaying. I will be a healer, and love all things that grow and are not barren." And again she looked at Faramir. "No longer do I desire to be a queen," she said.

Then Faramir laughed merrily. "That is well," he said; "for I am not a king." . . .

And he took her in his arms and kissed her under the sunlit sky, and he cared not that they stood high upon the walls in the sight of many. And many indeed saw them and the light that shone about them as they came down from the walls and went hand in hand to the Houses of Healing.

And to the Warden of the Houses Faramir said: "Here is the Lady Éowyn of Rohan, and now she is healed." (3:243)

8   THE OLD KING

The archetype of the Old King can be said to represent the collective consciousness. This means that its image is a personification of the leading principles and values in a community, which the single members are brought up to believe in. But any such symbols can be worn down so that they no longer carry a convincing content.

It is typical that an individuation process contains motives pointing toward the necessity of a transformation. But the Old King archetype points toward a collective psychological situation in the cultures of Western societies.

In the introduction, I referred to the type of fairy tales that begin like this: "Once upon a time there was a king who had three sons." It is also typical that the queen is missing in the beginning of the tale but that in the end the youngest son wins a princess and becomes the new king. In such cases the resolution of the fairy tale is to renew the collective consciousness by balancing out the masculine one-sidedness.

In *The Lord of the Rings*, three old kings appear. All of them have lost their queens. The wife of Elrond, Celebriand, has gone west. The wives of Denethor of Gondor and King Théoden of Rohan are both dead. To this one can add the disappearance of the Entwives, and in the Shire, old Bilbo and Frodo after him both remained unmarried.

The lack of women in Middle-earth is a symbolic expression that we live in a time when hearts have grown cold and in the various lands is a shortage of growth and fruitfulness—and love. All of this amounts to a general stagnation personified in the one-sidedness of the rulers and the isolation of the different domains.

Elrond, the elf lord, has lived in Rivendell all through the Third Age. His house is a place of refuge for the tired and suppressed, and it is a treasury of wise counselors and deep knowledge. Elrond is a guardian of all the beautiful things that existed in the past three thousand years. Many elves live in Rivendell, along with other wise and strong beings belonging to all the races of Middle-earth. Isildur's heirs also live there as children and in old age, and Elrond keeps the secret of their descendence from the kings of Númenor. Elrond is clairvoyant and foresees that one will come from that kin who is destined to take a mighty part in the events of the future.

However, in the present time of *The Lord of the Rings* Elrond's court has been without a queen for more than five hundred years. Elrond's wife, Celebriand, was attacked by Sauron's people on her way to Lórien; she was tortured and received a wound that would not heal. The year after the attack, she left Middle-earth.

Despite all the beauty and poetry that the reader experiences in the House of Elrond through the eyes of the hobbits, Rivendell has become a kind of library, a refuge without dynamic. When Aragorn appeared as the long-awaited heir, Elrond understood with mild resignation that Aragorn's victory, at best, will lead to his own departure and his loss of Arwen.

Théoden and Denethor, whose names apart from an "r" are mirrors of each other, both lost a beloved son, and in different ways they both have become corrupted. Théoden has become so crippled by his spiritual impoverishment that, though once tall, he now looks like a dwarf. Gandalf sets him straight:

> "I bid you come out before your doors and look
> abroad. Too long have you sat in shadows and trusted
> to twisted tales and crooked promptings." (2:119)

Rohan's people are riders and warriors—a kind of idealized and stylized Vikings. Gandalf arouses the warrior-king in Théoden to a last deed. After the battle at Helm's Deep, he takes the king with him to Orthanc; on the road they see a group of Ents. Théoden is amazed and says:

> "Long we have tended our beasts and our fields, built
> our houses, wrought our tools, or ridden away to help
> in the wars of Minas Tirith. And that we called the
> life of Men, the way of the world. We cared little for
> what lay beyond the borders of our land. Songs we
> have that tell of these things, but we are forgetting
> them, teaching them only to children, as a careless
> custom. And now the songs have come down among
> us out of strange places, and walk visible under the
> Sun." (2:155)

The people of the Mark have this in common with the hobbits of the Shire and the men of Gondor—as well as the inhabitants in the real contemporary world—that they have neglected the wondrous and fantastic aspect of life, and they wrongly believe it belongs in the nursery room. This is an Old King attitude, a central matter for Tolkien as the author of *The Lord of the Rings*. And, interestingly, a central feature of the literary criticism of the book has been that it belonged to young readers.

Théoden himself becomes like a legend in his last ride:

> Fey he seemed, or the battle-fury of his fathers ran like new fire in his veins, and he was borne up on Snow-mane like a god of old, even as Oromë the Great in the battle of the Valar when the world was young. His golden shield was uncovered, and lo! it shone like an image of the Sun, and the grass flamed into green about the white feet of his steed ... and the hosts of Mordor wailed, and terror took them, and they fled, and died, and the hoofs of wrath rode over them. (3:113)

Oromë was named the god of war among the Valar in the *Silmarillion*, but this is the only time Tolkien uses the word *god* in *The Lord of the Rings*.

Théoden falls with great honor. That is not the case with Denethor, who is a much more complex person. Gondor, too, is going down but for deeper reasons.

> "Yet even so it was Gondor that brought about its own decay, falling by degrees into dotage, and thinking that the Enemy was asleep, who was only banished not destroyed," Faramir explains. (2:286)

Gondor's rulers, descendants of Númenor, still yearned for immortality even though this had brought about the fall of Númenor. They did not find it, and the last king died childless a thousand years before.

The point here is that if you fear death too much, you lose the fruitfulness of life, too. I shall return to this theme in a later chapter.

The men of Gondor and the Rohirrim became allies, and the simpler people of the Mark adopted some of Gondor's higher culture, but the people of Gondor also became more like the people of the Mark, no longer high, a twilight people. Théoden was seduced by Wormtongue/Saruman, but he could be healed by Gandalf. Denethor, who is older and much wiser, has fallen deeper and to the darkest enemy. Through the seer stone he is corrupted by Sauron himself, and he also has the misfortune to love the noblest son, Faramir, less.

At the end of the story, all three old kings are gone. Théoden and Denethor are both dead, and Elrond has sailed away to Valinor.

As in the fairy-tale pattern, three young lords have replaced the old kings, and they have each won a bride: in the united kingdoms, Aragorn rules with Arwen. Éomer becomes king in Rohan and marries the daughter of Prince Imrahil of Dol Amroth, whose sister was the wife of Denethor. Faramir becomes the steward of Ithilien with his bride Éowyn. They are all knitted together in kinship and friendship. And to these three couples, we must add the fourth: the hobbit couple Sam and Rose in the Shire.

Psychologically, this means that a new and better balance has been reached in the collective consciousness. The men who take over are able to give and take in friendship and love; and they are both learned in lore and the arts and able to take action when needed.

9   THE SPIRIT

The spirit was originally thought of as something in the shape of a human or an animal who met the individual as an other. Tolkien makes use of this idea when he explains in the *Silmarillion* that the Valar and Maiar are spirits who dress themselves in bodies just like humans dress in clothes, and who, in such bodily shapes, met with elves and men.

When the spirit appears in fairy tales or dreams as an archetypal image, it is often as the wise old man (Jung 1948, par. 396). The Danish word for spirit is *ånd*, and the word for breath, *ånde*, is almost identical. The same is true in many languages. Not only living things breathe, the wind does so, too, and spirit is often associated with the wind and with beings of flight and speed. The eagles are the allies of Gandalf, and Shadowfax runs like the wind; Saruman has birds as spies and messengers. Everything about the archetypal spirit is personified in both good and evil aspects in the two wizards Gandalf and Saruman. Together they represent the alchemical *Mercurius Duplex*.

The spirit as a positive principle is what gives life, stimulates, inspires, ignites, and unites. The spirit is a dynamic principle, life as opposed to death. Traditionally, we consider spirit to be counter to nature, but this is caused by mechanical thinking. Living nature, of course, is not opposed to the spirit but is a part of it. The true opposite of spirit is dead nature; or a way of thinking of nature as being just dead matter.

Saruman is actually demonstrating his spiritual fall through his violent attacks on nature; the landscapes around Orthanc have become barren and poisonous, and his orcs are cutting down the trees without cause. Treebeard explains to Merry and Pippin: "He [Saruman] has a mind of metal and wheels; and he does not care for growing things, except as far as they serve him for the moment" (2:76).

In Tolkien's *Silmarillion*, we are told that Gandalf and Saruman really are spiritual beings; they are Maiar who rank a little lower than the Valar. Five wizards were sent to Middle-earth in the Third Age, when the power of Sauron grew again about two thousand years before the events in *The Lord of the Rings*. Only three of those wizards (in elf language *istari*, meaning wise) are named: Gandalf Greyhame, Saruman the White, and Radagast the Brown.

The wizards came over the sea to Middle-earth shaped as men, but they were never young and they age very slowly. They possessed mighty powers; the elves thought that they were sent from Valinor to resist Sauron and to unite everybody with the will to oppose him; but they were forbidden to meet his power with power or to try to win mastery over elves or men with force or fear (3:365). Gandalf always calls himself a counselor. After his transformation into the White Rider, however, he wields great power.

In the year 2463 of the Third Age, Galadriel called the White Council together for the first time. Besides herself, the members were Elrond, Cirdan, Gandalf, Saruman, and a number of other elf lords. It was the wish of Galadriel that Gandalf should take on its leadership, but he refused because he did not wish to have any formal bond to anybody but those who sent him. Then Saruman became the chief of the Council (1999, p. 300), so the White Council was not a wizard's council, and Saruman was never Gandalf's superior.

From the beginning, Saruman envied Gandalf, for he was proud and imperious. Treebeard thinks that Saruman already at that time had gone astray (2:76). Before long, Saruman began to look for the Ring of Power for himself, and he misled the other members of the Council. Then he withdrew into Isengard, which he turned into a stronghold. He began to spy on Gandalf's movements, and he sent secret agents to Bree and Southfarthing (3:370).

When Gandalf is summoned by Saruman, he realizes that something is all wrong. Saruman has changed his name to Saruman the Wise, Saruman the Ring-maker, Saruman of Many Colours—his mantle is now of changing colors and he carries a magic ring on his finger (1:272). Saruman appeals to Gandalf, suggesting that the two of them form an alliance, now that the power of the Dark Lord is growing. Here we see a central feature of the negative side of the archetypal spirit, the spiritual seduction:

> "the Wise, such as you and I, may with patience come
> at last to direct its courses, to control it. We can bide
> our time, we can keep our thoughts in our hearts,
> deploring maybe evils done by the way, but approving
> the high and ultimate purpose: Knowledge, Rule,
> Order. . . ." (1:272)

Of course, Saruman's real purpose is to make Gandalf reveal the whereabouts of the Master Ring. Gandalf understands that Saruman has been completely overtaken by Mordor, even though he does not know it himself.

Saruman takes Gandalf prisoner. However, he is freed by Gwaihir, the lord of the winds, and carried to Rohan, where Shadowfax is loaned to him, and he reaches Rivendell shortly before Frodo.

There is a difference between the evils of Saruman and those of Sauron. Tolkien, however, points out the connection:

> For all those arts and subtle devices, for which he forsook his former wisdom, and which fondly he imagined were his own, came but from Mordor; so that what he made was naught, only a little copy, a child's model or a slave's flattery, of that vast fortress, armoury, prison, furnace of great power, Barad-dûr, the Dark Tower, which suffered no rival, and laughed at flattery, biding its time, secure in its pride and its immeasurable strength. (2:160–61)

Human consciousness seems to have changed somewhat in the course of history. A number of psychic phenomena that today are considered to be located within the mind were originally experienced by our ancestors as something partly outside themselves, as in the famous opening lines of the *Iliad:* "Sing, O goddess, the anger of Achilles son of Peleus, that brought countless ills upon the Achaeans." Achilles was not really seen as the agent of these ills, but rather the anger was the agent. Today, when we are "beside ourselves" or "out of our minds" in the grip of some affect, the words we use to describe it are considered metaphors. We are expected to master impulse control in the normal course of development.

So also with the spirit. In everyday language, the word is most often used to refer to a set of sensible and rational guidelines. Taking Saruman as an example, we can see that sometimes it is from the seemingly sensible and rational that seduction and self-deceit spring. Saruman's voice is his strongest magic; everything he says sounds so right and reasonable.

Jung discusses the "enlightened rationalist" and his self-deceit in "The Phenomenology of the Spirit in Fairytales" (1948). Rhetorically he asks if rational reduction has led to the beneficial control of matter and spirit. The answer, as he sees it in the shadow of World War II, is obvious:

> man has been delivered from no fear, a hideous
> nightmare lies upon the world ... already we are
> fascinated by the possibilities of atomic fission
> and promise ourselves a Golden Age—the surest
> guarantee that the abomination of desolation will
> grow to limitless dimensions. (par. 454)

All of this, Jung argues, is caused by the human spirit which is completely unconscious of the demonism that clings to it. This attitude only maintains the mutual projections so that somebody else is always to blame for the new wars to happen. This quote could be a comment on the figure of Saruman:

> It seems to me ... that mankind, because of its
> scientific and technological development, has in

increasing measure delivered itself over to the danger of possession. True, the archetype of the spirit is capable of working for good as well as for evil, but it depends upon man's free—i.e., conscious—decision whether the good also will be perverted into something satanic. (Ibid., par. 455)

Saruman, as he was originally, represents a spirit of science. In elf language his name means "he who can." In the good sense, this kind of spirit serves truth and knowledge.

As for the spirit personified in the figure of the wise old man, surely there is more to wisdom than knowledge. Saruman was more clever and cunning than wise. I have described wisdom as the aim of individuation (Skogemann 1992, p. 156). But only in recent years has wisdom come into the focus of more systematic psychological research. A set of criteria have been set up to describe it; these are (a) rich factual knowledge about human nature and the life course; (b) rich procedural knowledge about ways of dealing with life problems; (c) lifespan contextualism, that is, an awareness and understanding of the many contexts of life, how they relate to each other and change over the lifespan; (d) value relativism and tolerance, that is, an acknowledgment of individual, social, and cultural differences in values and life priorities; and (e) knowledge about handling uncertainty, including the limits of one's own knowledge and the knowledge of the world at large.[3]

In *The Lord of the Rings*, wisdom is distributed among more than one figure, although Gandalf is the most prominent. But even Gandalf would be corrupted by the Master Ring, as we hear when Frodo, in the beginning, asks him to take the Ring:

> "No!" cried Gandalf, springing to his feet. "With that power I should have power too great and terrible. And over me the Ring would gain a power still greater and more deadly." His eyes flashed and his face was lit as by a fire within. "Do not tempt me! For I do not wish to become like the Dark Lord himself. Yet the way of the Ring to my heart is by pity, pity for weakness and the desire of strength to do good. Do not tempt me! I dare not take it, not even to keep it safe, unused. The wish to wield it would be too great for my strength. I shall have such need of it. Great perils lie before me." (1:70–71)

When Elrond appoints the Fellowship of the Ring, Gandalf is his first choice: "With you and your faithful servant, Gandalf will go; for this shall be his great task, and maybe the end of his labours" (1:289).

The Gandalf we meet in the first book does not, however, represent the whole truth about him. A qualitative leap happens to Gandalf after his death and rebirth. In Moria, he meets the Balrog, his "equal." The Balrog is also a spirit, namely one of those Maiar who served the evil Melkor in the oldest times. When Gandalf blocks his road on the bridge, he says something strange: "I am a servant of the Secret Fire, wielder of the flame of Anor" (1:344). *Anor* means "the sun." The secret fire may refer to the imperishable flame of Ilúvatar (Tolkien 1999, p. 4). Interestingly, the "secret fire" is also an alchemical expression for the hidden spiritual principle in matter.

Gandalf destroys the Balrog, but he dies himself and is sent back into the world again naked (see the description of the battle, page 63).

> "There I lay staring upward, while the stars wheeled over, and each day was as long as a life-age of the earth. Faint to my ears came the gathered rumour of all lands: the springing and the dying, the song and the weeping, and the slow everlasting groan of overburdened stone." (2:106)

There he is found by Gwaihir, who has come at the bidding of Galadriel (the one other prominent wisdom figure in the story). Gwaihir remarks that Gandalf has become light as a swan's feather—he could probably float upon the wind—and the sun is shining right through him. Gandalf's physical body has become spiritualized. Galadriel heals him and dresses him in white, and Gandalf goes to Fangorn. At this point, there are several scenes where Saruman and Gandalf are mixed up because of the white robe. As Aragorn, Legolas, and Gimli meet Gandalf, Tolkien keeps the reader believing that this is Saruman enchanting the friends with his voice; the group even tries to attack him but their weapons fall helpless to the ground or catch on fire. They recognize him only then he says:

> "none of you have any weapon that could hurt me. Be merry! We meet again. At the turn of the tide. The great storm is coming, but the tide has turned." (2:98)

This is the turning point of the story, the promise that everything will be okay in the end, even if it first gets worse. Gandalf's white robe is shining and his eyes "bright, piercing as the rays of the sun" (2:98). Finally, the group recognizes him. Legolas calls him by his elf name, but when the others call him "Gandalf," he can hardly remember that name. He is different from what he was before:

"Yes, I am white now," said Gandalf. "Indeed I *am* Saruman, one might almost say, Saruman as he should have been." (2:98)

Obviously, the original ban on the wizards against using power and force is revoked in regard to Gandalf. Saruman broke it; and Saruman is about to be destroyed at the same time Gandalf returns as the White Rider:

"Do I not say truly, Gandalf," said Aragorn at last, "that you could go whithersoever you wished quicker than I? And this I also say: you are our captain and our banner. The Dark Lord has Nine. But we have One, mightier than they: the White Rider. He has passed through the fire and the abyss, and they shall fear him. We will go where he leads." (2:104)

Gandalf calls his white horse:

"That is Shadowfax. He is the chief of the *Mearas*, lords of horses, and not even Théoden, King of Rohan, has ever looked on a better. Does he not shine like silver, and run as smoothly as a swift stream? He has come for me: the horse of the White Rider. We are going to battle together." (2:108)

While Gandalf's human body has become spiritualized, his "natural body" is instead symbolized through Shadowfax. He doesn't exactly grow wings, but in the rest of the story, we see him rushing like a wind from one place to another, organizing, reviving, and uniting the various groups against Sauron.

At the court of King Théoden, Gandalf is at first unwelcome as Gandalf Stormcrow, one who is always bringing evil tidings. But Gandalf answers:

> "Yet in two ways may a man come with evil tidings.
> He may be a worker of evil; or he may be such as
> leaves well alone, and comes only to bring aid in time
> of need." (2:117)

Gandalf heals Théoden from the spiritual decay he has fallen into through his traitorous counselor, Wormtongue. Gratefully, the king gives him Shadowfax as a present:

> "Here now I name my guest, Gandalf Greyhame,
> wisest of counselors, most welcome of wanderers, a
> lord of the Mark, a chieftain of the Eorlingas while
> our kin shall last; and I give to him Shadowfax, prince
> of horses."
>
> "I thank you, Théoden King," said Gandalf. Then
> suddenly he threw back his grey cloak, and cast aside
> his hat, and leaped to horseback. He wore no helm
> nor mail. His snowy hair flew free in the wind, his
> white robes shone dazzling in the sun.
>
> "Behold the White Rider!" cried Aragorn, and all
> took up the words. (2:129)

Gandalf soon leaves the army of Théoden, but he promises to return at Helm's Deep. At the height of the battle, when Théoden attempts a last attack and the trees from Fangorn are threatening the vast orc army, Gandalf appears from the west with Erkenbrand and his men, and his red shield is lit by the rising sun:

> Down leaped Shadowfax, like a deer that runs
> surefooted in the mountains. The White Rider was
> upon them, and the terror of his coming filled the
> enemy with madness. The wild men fell on their faces
> before him. The Orcs reeled and screamed and cast
> aside both sword and spear. Like a black smoke driven
> by a mounting wind they fled. Wailing they passed
> under the waiting shadow of the trees; and from that
> shadow none ever came again. (2:147)

Gandalf has not only become white, he has become something more than a wizard. A comparison with the mythology of the archangel Michael lies at hand. He is the general of the Lord who, in Christian mythology, fights the dragon of Satan. Michael is, above all, the angel to count on when the servants of God are in trouble—he is also the one who comforts and strengthens and heals (Hansen 1996, p. 155). He is thought of as the moving power of God in the world, and from time to time he is even identified with the Holy Spirit (ibid., p. 281).

The reference to Michael, who became the guardian angel of England under the name of Saint George, is quite conscious on the part of Tolkien, I believe, as he has Faramir explain to Frodo: "This Mithrandir was, I now guess, more than a lore-master: a great mover of the deeds that are done in our time" (2:279).

Finally there is a confrontation between Gandalf and Saruman in Orthanc. We see Saruman in vain trying to persuade Gandalf and King Théoden's company. At last Gandalf offers to allow Saruman to come down and go freely.

> A shadow passed over Saruman's face; then it went
> deathly white. Before he could conceal it, they saw
> through the mask the anguish of a mind in doubt,
> loathing to stay and dreading to leave its refuge. For
> a second he hesitated, and no one breathed. Then he
> spoke, and his voice was shrill and cold. Pride and
> hate were conquering him. (2:187)

So Saruman rejects Gandalf's offer. Gandalf casts him out of the Order and out of the Council and breaks his staff. Desperately, Wormtongue throws the palantir after them, and Gandalf realizes the method by which Saruman has been seduced by Sauron.

Gandalf travels on to Gondor, where he tries to influence another powerful master, the steward Denethor, into gazing a little beyond his own interests:

> "But I will say this: the rule of no realm is mine,
> neither in Gondor nor any other, great or small. But
> all worthy things that are in peril as the world now
> stands, those are my care. And for my part, I shall not
> wholly fail of my task, though Gondor should perish,
> if anything passes through this night that can still grow
> fair or bear fruit and flower again in days to come. For
> I also am a steward. Did you not know?" (3:30–31)

If Gandalf is a steward, then who is his king? The Valar queen Varda, maybe, or even the One.

When Denethor goes mad, Gandalf takes the command in Minas Tirith and keeps up the morale: "Wherever he came men's hearts would lift again, and the winged shadow pass from memory" (3:98). But the attack on the gate of Minas Tirith is strong. The army is led by the Nazgûl captain. Grond, a giant ram in the shape of a hideous wolf, breaks through the wall. The White and the Black Rider confront each other:

> In rode the Lord of the Nazgûl . . . under the archway that no enemy ever yet had passed, and all fled before his face.
>
> All save one. There waiting, silent and still in the space before the Gate, sat Gandalf upon Shadowfax . . . .
>
> "You cannot enter here," said Gandalf, and the huge shadow halted. "Go back to the abyss prepared for you! Go back! Fall into the nothingness that awaits you and your Master. Go!"
>
> The Black Rider flung back his hood, and behold! he had a kingly crown; and yet upon no head visible was it set. The red fires shone between it and the mantled shoulders vast and dark. From a mouth unseen there came a deadly laughter.
>
> "Old fool!" he said. "Old fool! This is my hour. Do you not know Death when you see it? . . ."
>
> Gandalf did not move. And in that very moment, away behind in some courtyard of the City, a cock crowed. (3:102–3)

The cock crowing is a widespread symbol of the victory of life over death as light conquers night at dawn, and help arrives at this time.

After this victory Gandalf suggests that whatever army the allies can assemble goes directly against Sauron, even though it is likely that they all perish "far from the living lands" (3:156).

> "But we must at all costs keep his [Sauron's] Eye from
> his true peril. We cannot achieve victory by arms, but
> by arms we can give the Ring-bearer his only chance,
> frail though it be" (3:156)

As the battle rages before Barad-dûr, the defeat seems to be certain; but then Gandalf raises his hands and cries: "The Eagles are coming!" They come in long rows from the north and bear down on the Nazgûl like a heavenly host (3:226). In that moment the Ring falls into the fire of Mount Doom. On the plain Gandalf yells, "This is the hour of doom." And he bids the king of eagles, Gwaihir, and his brothers Landroval and Meneldor to find Frodo and Sam and save them.

Sam's first comment, as he wakes up in the House of Healing, is:

> "Gandalf! I thought you were dead! But then I
> thought I was dead myself. Is everything sad going to
> come untrue? What's happened to the world?"
> "A great Shadow has departed," said Gandalf, and
> then he laughed, and the sound was like music, or like
> water in a parched land. (3:230)

Later, Pippin says about Gandalf that now he laughs more than he talks. Gandalf's "work" is over. Although Gandalf is the one member of the Company who stays the longest with the hobbits, he finally says goodbye at the border of the Shire:

> "You must settle its affairs yourselves; that is what you
> have been trained for. Do you not yet understand?
> My time is over: it is no longer my task to set things
> to rights, nor to help folk to do so. And as for you, my
> dear friends, you will need no help. You are grown up
> now. Grown indeed very high; among the great you
> are, and I have no longer any fear at all for any of you."
> (3:275)

Then Gandalf turns aside to visit and talk with Tom Bombadil, and the reader meets him again only at the Grey Havens at the final departure.

10   THE ONE RING AND THE THREE ELVEN RINGS

The Master Ring is the strongest single symbol in the story, and Sauron is the title character in *The Lord of the Rings*. He is a Maia like Gandalf and Saruman. The spirits can take on bodies as they see fit, and Sauron has in older ages appeared as wolf, snake, or vampire and even at times in an attractive and beautiful shape. He did that at the time he crafted the Ring.

But in the age of the story, he does not seem to use a particular physical body. He uses other beings as hands, mouth, or eyes: the nine Ringwraiths seem to function as his nine fingers—he only has nine since Isildur chopped off the finger with the Ring in the last great battle in the Second Age. This evokes an image of the great shadow stretching its hands greedily out over the world spreading terror and hopelessness everywhere. Before the last battle, the officer of Barad-dûr Tower calls himself the Mouth of Sauron. However, Sauron's essence seems especially to be expressed through his eye, which also is his mark, called the Red Eye, the Lidless Eye, or the Eye in the Black Tower, who never sleeps.

This is what Frodo sees in Galadriel's mirror:

In the black abyss there appeared a single Eye that slowly grew, until it filled nearly all the Mirror. So terrible was it that Frodo stood rooted, unable to cry out or to withdraw his gaze. The Eye was rimmed with fire, but was itself glazed, yellow as a cat's, watchful and intent, and the black slit of its pupil opened on a pit, a window into nothing. (1:379)

Frodo also sometimes dream about the Eye. The closer he and Sam get to Mount Doom, the heavier the Ring becomes, and in the end the Ring and the Eye become one as a wheel of fire. Sam tries to encourage Frodo by reminding him of the good things, but Frodo can't remember anymore:

"At least, I know that such things happened, but I cannot see them. No taste of food, no feel of water, no sound of wind, no memory of tree or grass or flower, no image of moon or star are left to me. I am naked in the dark, Sam, and there is no veil between me and the wheel of fire. I begin to see it even with my waking eyes, and all else fades." (3:215)

The Ring has magic effects such as invisibility when worn, and it induces immortality and works special bodily changes as we see with both Gollum and Bilbo. But especially it works on the mind from within. All the descriptions of the special temptation of the Ring psychologically point in the same direction: the Ring of Power creates a madness of grandiosity and paranoia, and it gradually deforms the personality. Many mythological predecessors exist, but this psychological aspect sets this ring apart and makes it clearly a twentieth-century symbol, as Shippey points out (2000, p. 117).

So what is the Ring a symbol of? O'Neill is not in doubt: a perfect golden ring "is the Self, the potential force that promises finally to make whole both hobbit and Middle-earth" (1979, p. 65). But the Ring does no such thing; Frodo is not made whole, and Middle-earth is saved only through the destruction of the Ring.

It is often overlooked that the archetype of the Self also has a dark side which is obviously at work here. If the ego identifies with the self, inflation arises, a narcissistic grandiosity, akin to the immediate effect of the Ring.

There is more to it, however. The Ring is called "evil." Anybody who carries the Ring comes close to the essence of Sauron's being—and he is undisputedly evil. He may do his work on the mind of the person who bears the Ring, but he is also to be perceived as a real, outer enemy. The Ring will eat away the benevolent forces within the person so that he withers away and becomes a dark and evil spirit, like the nine Ringwraiths. Sauron bends others to his will, so that only one will exists. He creates an evil order of dead nature and unlife in a void. The Ring and its master is a truly archetypal image of the dark side of the Self. Therefore we should also try to locate the light side of the Self in the universe of Middle-earth.

As the One Ring literally overshadows everything else, it is easy to forget that the Third Age in Middle-earth, until the present time of our story, was upheld by the three "good" elven rings, while the One Ring was in hiding. The guardians of the three rings are Galadriel, Elrond, and Gandalf.

Only Galadriel owned her ring from the time it was forged in the middle of the Second Age. All the Great Rings were perfected ten years before Sauron forged the One Ring. The elf lords soon detected his intentions, and they hid the three rings before Sauron realized where they were or who owned them.

After Sauron's fall at the end of the Second Age, the One Ring disappeared, and then the great elf rings were wielded, though it was still a secret as to who owned them. Elrond inherited his from Gil-Galad, and both Galadriel and Elrond upheld their magic elven kingdoms in Lórien and Rivendell by means of their rings, Nenya and Vilya. Nobody but Galadriel herself ever wielded her ring. Gandalf was given his ring, Narya, by Cirdan in the Grey Havens when he arrived in Middle-earth a thousand years into the Third Age. Only Galadriel and Elrond knew that the wizards had come over the sea, and only the two of them and Cirdan knew that Gandalf had been given the red ring (O'Neill 1979, p. 299).

The three great rings are set with gems: Galadriel's with a white stone, Elrond's with a blue stone, and Gandalf's with a red stone. The gems are associated with the four elements as the philosophers of antiquity and the Middle Age alchemists knew them, that is, air, water, and fire. Sauron's ring has no stone, but it must logically represent the lacking element, earth. Sauron's color is certainly black, and he is always connected with heavy matter such as stone and iron. His fire is a "dark" fire, like the one surrounding the Balrog in the mines of Moria. Whereas Gandalf serves the creating fire, Sauron serves the fire of destruction—that which is burning the strongest in Mount Doom.

The four rings together form a collective Self symbol in Middle-earth all through the Third Age. The situation is similar to that with which Jung (1951) concludes in his analysis of the Christian age in the light of alchemical symbolism, with the good Trinity and Satan or the Antichrist as the hidden fourth.

The good rings can uphold the status quo; but there is no dynamic of creativity. Just like the symbol of collective consciousness, which I discussed in chapter 1, the symbol of the collective Self is also worn down.

Jung says about the mandala pictures of his patients that they, like magic circles, bind the lawless powers that belong the world of darkness and that they depict or create an order which transforms chaos to cosmos. Sauron's ring works like that, too, but in the opposite fashion: "One Ring to bring them all and in the darkness bind them." It represents the backside of the mandala, the dangerous element that comes forth if the individuation process gets stuck and the self is not realized and remains unconscious. This is what has happened in Middle-earth—as a mirror of our modern world.

Tolkien's use of the four elements is in a striking way related to the philosophy of the alchemists. They are the *prima materia*—components that hide in metals or other substances and are supposed to become united through the alchemical procedure so that the *lapis philosophorum*, the philosopher's stone, can appear. In their original condition, they coexist or are hostile to each other. The stone is also called *filius macrocosmi* and is thought to be alive, an Anthropos who is a redeemer and a parallel to Christ (Jung 1951, par.

375). In *The Lord of the Rings*, the stone, elfstone, unites and renews the elements.

Tolkien's mythology, as expressed in the *Silmarillion*, is only hinted at in *The Lord of the Rings* and its appendices. It is, however, not difficult to see that the dynamics of the Third Age are led by Sauron and his will to power. The wizards, Istari, were sent from Valinor as a countermove, and possibly also the hobbits who awaken into history around the same time. But the Istari were carefully instructed not to use power.

Sauron, and before him Melkor, has a will to subdue the whole world. Such a determination is practically nonexistent with the elves. Already the Valar were inclined to yield to Melkor. Determination is normally seen as a function of a well-developed ego. The basic psychological problem in Tolkien's world is to differentiate a "good" strength of will, one that is able to pursue and hold on to a goal, from an "evil" will to power. Considering the world as we know it, this seems a hopeless project because power is so corruptive. At the same time, it looks as though all rulers are capable of imagining that whatever they do is in the service of the good (Shippey 2000, p. 115).

Aragorn succeeds in this project because his goal is love, not power. He can stick with his goal even after obtaining power, however, only because the Ring is destroyed.

When Sauron's Ring is gone, the powers of the three elf rings go too. This is not really logical, as they were not made together, but on a psychological level it makes sense. In an individuation process, consciousness separates itself from the unconscious, and so there is a bittersweet parting from the magical world, symbolized by the elves leaving Middle-earth. The archetypes may not lose their ability to fascinate but the obsessive character of the unconscious recedes.

11   THE COLLECTIVE SHADOW

In Tolkien's creation myth, *Ainulindalë*, which is told in the *Silmarillion*, we hear how evil came into the world even before it was made while the Ainur sang their perfect song to the One.

> But as the theme progressed, it came into the heart of Melkor to interweave matters of his own imagining that were not in accord with the theme of Ilúvatar; for he sought therein to increase the power and glory of the part assigned to himself. To Melkor among the Ainur had been given the greatest gifts of power and knowledge, and he had a share in all the gifts of his brethrens. He had gone often alone into the void places seeking the Imperishable Flame; for desire grew hot within him to bring into Being things of his own, and it seemed to him that Ilúvatar took no thought for the Void, and he was impatient of its emptiness. Yet he found not the Fire, for it is with Ilúvatar. But being alone he had begun to conceive thoughts of his own unlike those of his brethren. (1999, p. 4)

A similar desire is known from the biblical myth about the grandiose angel, Lucifer, who was cast out of heaven. But in Tolkien's version, two psychological conditions are added as crucial before the desire develops into evilness and these are emptiness and loneliness. Melkor walks in chaos in the original Greek meaning of the word, which is the ether, the void—it is not mere disorder, such as a traffic jam.

As the story is told in the *Silmarillion*, the fighting between Melkor and the Valar occurs in endless waves. When the elves "awaken," they too are involved, and so are men as they step into history, now with Sauron as the enemy.

Every time the Valar take action, the result is that mountains raise or fall, lands sink into the sea, rivers change their course, and volcanos belch forth fire. On one hand, this is similar to the geological history of Earth, but on the other hand it can be seen as a description of a restless unconscious wherein all kinds of affective powers exist. An individual obsessed with rage, for instance, may dream about volcanos or landslides. In the *Silmarillion*, thousands of years roll on this way. It is relevant as background for *The Lord of the Rings*, but in the *Silmarillion* there is no conscious perspective and no psychological development. Such a perspective only comes into existence when the Ring is found by a hobbit.

Sauron's presence and his searching for his Ring in *The Lord of the Rings* highlights the difference between good and evil. To learn and know the difference and act on it is crucial for all the characters. When Frodo is sitting on the Seat of Sight and tries to decide what to do, he tells himself:

> "This at least is plain: the evil of the Ring is already
> at work even in the Company, and the Ring must

leave them before it does more harm. I will go alone."
(1:417–18)

The evil at work is obvious in that Boromir has just tried to take the Ring by force. But Frodo is also thinking that the Company has been split in regard to the individual members' ideas about its further course. Friend striving with friend and confusion about loyalties is the work of the enemy. Frodo himself almost gives in, as he takes on the Ring and feels the Eye searching for him:

> He heard himself crying out: *Never, never!* Or was it: *Verily I come, I come to you?* He could not tell. Then as a flash from some other point of power there came to his mind another thought: *Take it off! Take it off! Fool, take it off! Take off the Ring!* (1:417)

Frodo does not know that Gandalf is actually fighting with Sauron to help him; he experiences this as an inner conflict. Psychologically this corresponds to dreams where the self manifests itself as a voice of authority. Frodo is in a dreamlike, visionary state. At the same time, this is one of the places in *The Lord of the Rings* where the powers of light and darkness, good and evil, are obviously both inner and outer forces.

An ambiguity is present all through Tolkien's description of evil and the Ring, as Tom Shippey points out. On one hand, the Ring is an inner power that enhances all the negative sides existing in the psyche; this corresponds on a religious level to the Christian dogma that evil is "only" absence of good, *privatio boni* (Shippey 2000, p. 135).[4] All evil comes from man alone while God is only good.

On the other hand, the Ring seems to have its own will and aim, and Sauron is not only a shadow figure, but a Lord of Darkness and the creator of the Ring. The experiences of the twentieth century seemed to indicate that evil exists as a power in itself. For many centuries, this dualistic view has been considered a Christian heresy. But, Shippey continues, looking at Frodo's real defeat on Mount Doom one must ask: Was Frodo guilty? Did he give in to temptation? Or was he simply overpowered by evil?

> If one puts the questions like that, there is surprising and ominous echo to them, which suggests that this whole debate between "Boethian" and "Manichaean" views, far from being one between orthodoxy and heresy, is at the absolute heart of the Christian religion itself. (2000, p. 141)[5]

In *Ainulindalë*, it looks like Tolkien allows his one god to take the responsibility for both good and evil. When Melkor brought evil into the world, the One told him:

> "And thou, Melkor, shalt see that no theme may be played that hath not its uttermost source in me, nor can any alter the music in my despite. For he that attempteth this shall prove but mine instrument in the devising of things more wonderful, which he himself hath not imagined." (Tolkien 1999, p. 17)

Just before he said this, the One performed the violent theme of Melkor with his left hand, while the beautiful themes came from his right hand.

In his book, *Answer to Job* (1952), Jung also criticized the *privatio boni* dogma. In the foreword, he reminds the reader that the church father Clement, who lived before the heresy of Mani, taught that God rules the world with right and left hand. The right hand is Christ, the left is Satan. It seems to me not unlikely that Tolkien was inspired by this same image when he composed his creation scenario. Jung thought that as long as Christianity claims to be monotheistic, accepting that the opposites both are in God is unavoidable. This is what Jung saw mirrored in the story of Job: Job expected help from God against God—and he was rewarded.

If we now return to my hypothesis that the fascination of *The Lord of the Rings* stems from the condition of the collective unconscious in Western culture in our present time, and that Sauron and the Ring express the collective and archetypal shadow, of which we all carry a part—can we get closer to that shadow?

GENOCIDE AND THE HEART OF DARKNESS

Mordor (mòr-dòr), murder, mass murder, genocide: the murderer truly unites death and evil. It is obvious that Tolkien basically presents here an archetypal, primitive image of evil. In all cultures, the struggle for breath and other sufferings of a dying person have been interpreted as a fight with an invisible evil enemy, death.

The contemporary events that took place while Tolkien was working on *The Lord of the Rings*, that is, World War II and Nazism, carry the face of Mordor, of course, but *The Lord of the Rings* is not a political allegory. However, if we are going to examine the collective shadow as a psychological phenomenon, we cannot avoid the political world altogether, and we must expect repressions, denials, and projections, individually as well as collectively. Lindqvist (1996) and, more recently, Enzo Striderzo (2003) have pointed out that it is not possible to understand the Holocaust by examining the history of anti-Semitism alone nor by turning toward Stalin's Russia. We have to look west, toward "ourselves" to find the roots of the systematic genocides in Europe in the ages of discovery, capitalism, and colonialism.

Jung had an opportunity to meet Europeans as seen for the first time through the eyes of a stranger when he talked to the chief of the Taos pueblos, Ochwiä Biano. Biano thought that whites looked cruel with their thin lips and staring gazes, restless and always searching for something. He thought that the white people were mad. Biano's description provoked a long stream of images in Jung:

> I felt rising within me like a shapeless mist something
> unknown and yet deeply familiar. And out of this
> mist, image upon image detached itself: first Roman
> legions smashing into the cities of Gaul, and the
> keenly incised features of Julius Caesar, Scipio
> Africanus, and Pompey. I saw the Roman eagle on
> the North Sea and on the banks of the White Nile.
> Then I saw St. Augustine transmitting the Christian
> creed to the Britons on the tips of Roman lances,
> and Charlemagne's most glorious forced conversions
> of the heathen; then the pillaging and murdering
> bands of the Crusading armies. . . . Then followed

Columbus, Cortes, and the other conquistadors who with fire, sword, torture, and Christianity came down upon even these remote pueblos dreaming peacefully in the Sun, their Father. I saw, too, the peoples of the Pacific islands decimated by firewater, syphilis, and scarlet fever . . . .

What we from our point of view call colonization, missions to the heathen, spread of civilization, etc., has another face—the face of a bird of prey. (1961b, p. 248)

The situation became really awful during the nineteenth century. The combination of far-reaching guns and Darwin's theories about evolution transformed into ideas about the so-called lower races confronted by the colonial masters of Europe led to bestial and unscrupulous genocides in Africa, Tasmania, the Americas, and elsewhere. It became a widespread notion that these lower races—the black people, the Tasmanians, the Red Indians—after all were doomed by evolution. The white race was superior and therefore the other races had to perish (Lindqvist 1996, p. 123).

Some writers tried to express this new form of evil in a new form of literature, the fantastic. R. B. Cunninghame Graham, in "Higginson's Dream" (1928), told a story about the last battles between the whites and the natives on Tenerife. The natives, the *guanches*, were stricken by a weird illness that cost more lives than the fighting. This illness was called "modorra." To Cunninghame Graham, it was the white man's presence in and of itself that killed the natives, not because they suffered from a biological inferiority but because of the demands from the whites that they instantly adapt to a special version of European culture—gin, the Bible, and guns.

In *The Invisible Man* by H. G. Wells (1897), a scientist invents a method to become invisible. Soon he begins to exploit the situation: because no one can see him, he can without risk commit the worst deeds of violence, and he can kill anybody who stands in his way. No one can prevent him. He becomes nonhuman, a complete egoist. This figure laid the foundation for the modern serial killer in literature. In Well's last and most famous book, *The War of the Worlds* (1898), London is attacked by a superior race from Mars. Slowly they sweep London in a cloud of black smoke, an impenetrable, poisonous darkness. Orson Welles, in 1938, caused thousands of people to flee from New Jersey when they mistook his radio version of the novel for actual reality.

The most unsettling among such books, however, is Joseph Conrad's *The Heart of Darkness* (1902). The young Marlow works as a captain of a steamboat on the Congo River and sails to the utmost outpost of civilization, a trading station deep in the "heart of darkness." On the journey, Marlow begins to understand the backside, that is, the shadow, of civilization. He—and the reader—meet the darkness in themselves, so to speak. The representatives in the colonies were invisible, like Wells's scientist—both in the sense that their weapons killed with ease and at a distance, and in the sense that no one at home could see what they were doing. They were separated from ordinary civilization by the dense jungles and enormous distances as well as by lack of control and supervision. They could wield uninhibited power unhindered.

As it turned out, they would often be transformed in a way like Wells's invisible man; they murdered, tortured, and punished at random. *Heart of Darkness* used to be interpreted as a journey into the wildness of the mind, to the unconscious strata where the civilized European personality ceased to be, and where darkness, violence, and brutishness rule. This was personified in the description of the leader of the remote trading station, the demonic Kurtz.

Kurtz's mother is half English and his father is half French. He was the finest product of the European culture at that time. The international society for the suppression of savage customs has entrusted Kurtz to write a report for their guidance. Marlow reads it, and it is seventeen pages long, very elegantly written.

> "The opening paragraph, however, in the light of later
> information, strikes me now as ominous. He began
> with the argument that we whites, from the point
> of development we had arrived at, 'must necessarily
> appear to them [savages] in the nature of supernatural
> beings—we approach them with the might of a
> deity,' and so on, and so on. 'By the simple exercise
> of our will we can exert a power for good practically
> unbounded.'" (Conrad 1902, p. 123)

Marlow reads it with enthusiasm. There are no practical hints to interrupt the magic current of phrases, unless a kind of note at the foot of the last page, scrawled evidently much later, in an unsteady hand, may be regarded as the exposition of a method. It says: "Exterminate all the brutes!"

Heart of Darkness is a scary novel, but it is even more

scary that in recent years it has turned out to be based very closely on Conrad's own diary of a time when, as a young man, he worked on a steamboat on the Congo River, exactly like his character. *Heart of Darkness* is not a fantastic story but concrete reality.

Mordor is a true representation of the shadow of the white man in the nineteenth as well as the twentieth century. Officially, civilization was spread all over the world, but in reality systematic genocides were carried out. Eventually, the truth came to be known to the public. So Hitler knew about genocide; he did not invent it. Sven Lindqvist writes:

> Hitler was in his whole political life motivated by a fanatic hatred for Jews. His anti-Semitism belongs to a thousand-year tradition that often led to murder and mass murder of Jews. But the step from mass murder to genocide was only taken when the anti-Semitic tradition met the tradition of genocide that arose along with the European expansion in America, Australia, Africa and Asia. (1996, p. 180)

In Sudan, the native populations were reduced by 75 percent, in the Congo by 50 percent, and on Sri Lanka, 90 percent of the natives were murdered. The Tasmanians were exterminated.

During the twentieth century, the world was torn between the democratic states and the communist ones; no sooner had the communist side dissolved then the next opposition appeared in the twenty-first century: officially, it is the civilized world against terrorism; less officially, it is the Western nations against Islamism.

In totalitarian societies and fundamentalist religious or political systems we find the caricature of the archetype of the Self: absolute order, meaning, and wholeness. In Mao's China, as in Saddam Hussein's Iraq, there was one father god, one thought, one will, and any resistance, even if only in words, could lead to torture or death. Images of the omnipresent leader would be projected everywhere, on posters and on television, such that the people were bombarded with the archetypal life of the mythological culture hero. The fact that such societies existed and still exist in reality means that it is just that much easier to go on projecting the terrible shadow onto others.

This darkness in human nature is Mordor, wherever it appears. In his foreword to *The Lord of the Rings*, Tolkien comments on World War II:

> The real war does not resemble the legendary war in its process or its conclusion. If it had inspired or directed the development of the legend, then certainly the Ring would have been seized and used against Sauron; he would not have been annihilated but enslaved, and Barad-dûr would not have been destroyed but occupied. Saruman, failing to get possession of the Ring, would in the confusion and treacheries of the time have found in Mordor the missing links in his own researches into Ring-lore, and before long he would have made a Great Ring of his own with which to challenge the self-styled Ruler of Middle-earth. (1:7)

The Lord of the Rings is no mirror of the war—it is rather such that World War II and other wars prove that the Ring still exists. When the Iraqi war broke out, some people protested by hanging banners out of windows with the text: "Frodo failed his mission. Bush has the Ring!"

Sauron's Ring possesses anyone who carries it. To be possessed by the dark side of the self implies psychologically that the ego is sacrificed to a regressive merger with a group self, which induces unlimited greatness and power. At the same time, the conscious ability to think, feel, and act critically, rationally, and ethically is also sacrificed. It is a sick structure, psychologically as well as sociologically, that demands the total submission of the part for the aims of the whole. But this is what happens to the extreme to those persons and peoples who, in *The Lord of the Rings*, submit to Sauron or Saruman.

Jung thought at the problem of evil had become un-avoidable for Western man:

> Therefore the individual who wishes to have an answer to the problem of evil, as it is posed today, has need, first and foremost, of *self-knowledge*, that is, the utmost possible knowledge of his own wholeness. He must know relentlessly how much good he can do, and what crimes he is capable of, and must beware of regarding the one as real and the other as illusion. (1961b, p. 330)

Many people in the Western world have begun to realize that a lot of our problems are ethical, but simultaneously widespread feelings of helplessness exist. Their dimensions are aptly mirrored in the image of the small hobbit versus the mighty Dark Lord.

To destroy Sauron's Ring corresponds to the equally impossible task of exterminating the source of inhumanity, not the enemy, but in one's own psyche. The answer is not pacifism, although Frodo really becomes a pacifist; but he also becomes paralyzed, unable to act. In *The Lord of the Rings* there is no either-or. Merry, Pippin, Gimli, Legolas, and indeed Aragorn go to war in a fighting spirit. Although the real victory cannot be won by weapon, there are battles both before and after where weapons are used.

I have interpreted the symbol of the Ring as the dark part of the Self through real and literary examples of inhuman acts. We know that serial killers are psychopaths and that such persons have themselves been the victims of abuse early in their lives. But the effect of the Ring strikes everyone—just a bit slower the "better" the person is from the beginning.

Jungian analyst Donald Kalched (1996) introduced the concept of a self-care system, meaning that a person may have developed a pathological way to deal with self-regulation as well as regulation of relations to one's surroundings. Kalched claims that this self-care system is formed in answer to an early trauma, but later in life it works against all spontaneous, creative self-expression. In dreams and fantasies the self-care system portrays itself as an archetypal dyad in the shape of a powerful being and a vulnerable, young, innocent child or animal self. The powerful part acts as protector and/or persecutor of its vulnerable partner. Most frequently, the dream-I experiences it as frightening, murderous, or demonic, but sometimes it appears as protective and as a giver of special boons.

I suggest that the archetypal pattern of the self-care system can be understood in a general way, namely as a human readiness for dissociation that can be activated relatively easily under certain circumstances.

The phenomenon that in the 1970s became known as the Stockholm syndrome is a typical example. An astonished world, through the new visual mass media, became witnesses to a strange situation. Four hostages who were saved after six days of imprisonment in a bank in Stockholm actively resisted their saviors, and afterward they refused to testify against the bank robbers. Since then, it has been realized that similar reactions occurred with other hostages, and that it is in fact a general phenomenon. West and Martin (1994) have described situations in which not only hostages, but also prisoners of war, members of religious cults of the totalitarian type, and intelligence agents who have lived undercover a long time, were at risk of undergoing comprehensive transformation of personality. It is a dissociative phenomenon that is not related to childhood trauma. It is the kind of possession that occurs with the Ring, wherein the normal identity disappears and is taken over by the norms and values of the guardian or leader.

The syndrome can become active within a few days under conditions where the victim cannot escape, is isolated and threatened with death, but also is sometimes shown kindness by the guardian. The means to call forth this syndrome are similar to the means used by executors of political systems with strong totalitarian features.

12

THE END
OF AN
AGE

The Lord of the Rings is a narrative about the end of an age. What does that really mean? Some think that the end of the age equals the end of the world. Many have been contacted by missionaries, such as Jehovah's Witnesses, who are ready to tell you that the doomsday battle at Armageddon will occur soon.

We also meet secular versions of the prophecy that the end of the world is soon to come. They are rational and possible and therefore more convincing to most people: we shall perish in our own pollution after having used up all the resources of nature; we shall die of global hunger because of overpopulation; an atomic war will desolate the earth; changes in the climate will bring on the end of the world.

In *The Lord of the Rings*, there is nothing to indicate that Tolkien imagined that the world would come to an end if the Dark Lord won. Although Fire Mountain is called Mount Doom, this does not refer to doomsday in the biblical sense. The next age would simply be extremely unpleasant; psychologically one could say that the light of consciousness would be put out, overshadowed by unconscious darkness. Yes, the end of the world will take place—there are several references to it in *The Lord of the Rings*—but Tolkien does not mix it up with the problem of the age.

Historically, it is an old phenomenon to speculate about what will happen when a given age ends, and it is typical that people fluctuate between fears and hopes. In the science of religion such speculations are called eschatology, that is, the teachings of the end of times. How can one know the signs? How will all things perish and hopefully be transformed into something new and better? The world has survived the year 2000, but it is still under discussion as to whether the age has changed yet from Pisces to Aquarius. What interests me here is the general psychological expectation that the end of time is getting close and how this has been described in modern times in different literary stories, *The Lord of the Rings* being one of the most important and influential by far. A common feature among echatological novels is that their literary form is fantasy and also that a central theme is the archetypal one about the struggle between good and evil at the end of an age.

For a rather long period our Western culture has been dominated by a chronic belief in progress, and eschatology has not been very successful. But the Western world is no longer so optimistic. As the year 2000 passed, people in general were not as sure that things would be better in the present century as most people were when the nineteenth century ended. At that time, they were terribly wrong: the twentieth century was the most bloody and destructive ever. At this point, we could hope to be proved wrong in our fears.

In eschatology there are components other than the changing of the eon or the turn of a thousand years, even though the progress of time in cultures like the Western is so important. Cultures with a cyclical conception of time have no special interest in the idea of the last times.

In studying the history of religions, it is a striking fact that only those religions that were founded by a single prophet figure such as Zarathustra, Jesus, or Muhammad, also developed a real eschatology. In the nineteenth century, many messianic movements, also centered on prophetic figures, sprouted among nonliterary people around the world. A common feature was the belief that the power of the white man would be broken and the natives would win freedom and happiness. Such studies give the impression that eschatological ideas are the answers of religion to a situation which is deeply unsatisfying whether this concerns a general lack of roots in a community changing too fast, or whether the concern may be related to a spiritual uncertainty manifested in feelings of sin and insufficiency.

In eschatological ideas a longing is expressed, a longing for a place where there is freedom from conflicts, sufferings, and loss. Such longings are clearly archetypal. Throughout history, this wonderful place has been located in the beyond, in life after death, or in a future world appearing after the final destruction. A change of location seemed to occur, however, at the beginning of the nineteenth century. Now the paradise dream begins to appear as something that could happen in this life and in this world. Grundtvig, to whom I referred in the introduction, wrote a great religious poem in 1832, "I Know a Country." The whole poem expresses such ideas and emotions. In a poetic language, Grundtvig reflects on the origins in the child and the difficulty in the grownup of giving up the illusory part of the longings and the way they can be modified and contained in a mature religious attitude.

The strange thing about the poem is that it is not about life after death. It is a description of the longing for a paradise existing in this world, although it is also recognized as an illusion. We have this wonderful dream, which the romantic artists of the time tried to visualize in images and words. But the fact is that we still have to die.

Grundtvig's century, the nineteenth, was the century of the great -isms, for example, Marxism, which clearly held such expectations of a paradise on earth. The tendency has continued, but whoever is interested in old-fashioned paradise nowadays? People do not believe in it anymore—so of course the Western version of belief in reincarnation is spreading. Here you have an interpretation of death that, in effect, allows you to stay in this world forever, always improving. Modern believers in reincarnation must be the last refuge for the positivistic faith in evolution.

The "dream," the "longings"—of course, modern language is much different and the objects of the longings have changed as well into many different forms. There is a difference between the advertisement in the newspaper offering a seminar in self-realization and the television commercial showing the white beaches of a paradisiacal island with beautiful men and women drinking cool drinks. But both appeal to the psychological image of a condition of everlasting happiness and to a longing to reach it.

It is a universal idea that the quality of time decays by itself. The good time is worn out. All myths and stories about the great battle taking place at the end of time will have a description of the good beginning. Tolkien gives his version in the creation myth in the *Silmarillion*. In the beginning, everything is good. But soon there are mistakes, transgressions, crimes, sins. Decay begins. Death comes into the world. The world is bound to become worse and worse, and humans constantly have to renew it through cult and rituals and prayers. But they have not succeeded, as anybody can see. In Scandinavian mythology, we have a dramatic description of this in the poem, "Vølven's spådom," the prophecy of the Vølve, a seeress. It follows a typical pattern: in the beginning everything is well, but early on the wondrous golden tablets with which the gods play are lost. Then the tragic death of Baldr happens—a sure sign that Ragnarök is unavoidable. In the end, a great battle takes place, all gods and men are destroyed. And yet, after Ragnarök there appears a new heaven and a new earth; the golden tablets will be found again and new gods will take the place of the old. A single human couple will survive, and they and their lineage shall live happily ever after.

We modern enlightened people do not believe in Odin or Thor, nor in trolls or giants, unless of course they are figures in a fantasy story. We know so many things that our ancestors did not. We know that events have certain causes, and that influenza is not caused by demons or constellations of planets but by viruses. We even have a psychological explanation of demons from Jung: they represent unconscious processes, filling out all the voids of knowledge. We think mainly of the psychic as something inside humans. If psychic stuff happens to appear outside, as projections or projective identifications, we immediately must start working to get them back into place.

In ancient times people thought that the sins and mistakes and injustices of humankind literally piled up. Eventually there was such a large amount of badness that it led to destruction, as in the Old Testament when the Lord send a deluge over the world to clean it up.

Now we think everything is completely different. We can actually measure how the dirt is piling up. Our demons are called pollution, the greenhouse effect, ozone holes, and everything is concrete, material, and realistic. We know this to be objective and an actual threat to us all. We know. But we feel just as powerless as the Nordic gods after the death of Baldr. Maybe it is because we are almost as mighty as the old gods. Humanity has made itself lord over nature and over life and death in a way that is close to the powers of the Aesir.

What I want you to follow here is the idea that these things and events which are so real have a psychic aspect. We have not separated so much from the world as we believe. We are a part of the world and it is a part of us. Our mythological fantasy still works unceasingly and is a cocreator in our total view of the world.

I ask you to try to make a mental comparison between an older psychological universe and our own: our ancestors were, of course, just as sure of the existence of giants and trolls as we are of things we can measure. Demons were the real causes of the badness of the world. In old Scandinavia, the whole world was filled with life. Trolls and giants lived in the mountains, dwarfs and elves in the old barrows. Divine and demonic beings dwelled in dark moors, in the old trees, and in the holy springs.

All psychic powers were personified outside of humankind. The landscapes of the world outside the cultivated and orderly and inhabited community were neither politically, economically, nor even geographically conditioned, but rather mythologically structured. Even up to our time, folklore has taught that one was at serious risk of becoming spellbound by these powers if one walked alone in the night or outside the borders of the ordered community.

The end of this paradigm came slowly and in two stages. First, Christianity brought along the idea that the baptism of the child protected its spirit from the raw forces of nature. Together with this also came an attempt to empty nature of trolls and pixies and the like. When nature—so to speak—had been done away with, the natural sciences developed with the aim of controlling nature. So what we see now is an image of dead nature, where the ghostly waste piles up and up. As much as science used to be admired, and scientists regarded as half-divine persons, it is now regarded with deep ambivalence. High schools and universities are complaining about the declining number of students of the natural sciences.

We house many other demons. Think, for example, of the idea of hidden leaders of multinational companies, positioned like spiders in a web, impossible to catch or punish. We imagine anonymous, cold, impersonal powers that influence our lives and secretly rule our world to serve their own purposes. Such ideas are the subject of many films and novels and found often in the media. Who is able to say for sure what kind of reality is behind all these fantasies? Where does paranoid fantasy stop and reality begin?

The component of mythological fantasy is undoubtedly easier to see in its extreme versions, which fewer of us will identify as real. Parts of the modern UFO mythology have a terrifying demonic aspect. In earlier stories about meetings with extraterrestrial intelligence, these beings were met with positive and even messianic expectation. But this has changed in recent years. The phenomenon is called "alien abduction," the theory that some people have been abducted by extraterrestrial beings, but that they have repressed everything and will only remember the experience when they go into psychotherapy because of their psychic problems. They are treated with regression hypnosis; then they begin to remember how they were taken up in spaceships and examined by the aliens in a cold and clinical way. Their sex organs seemed to be of special interest, but also other organs, such as the brain. The victims felt powerless, molested, misused.

The similarity of alien abduction to the ancient idea of becoming spellbound is, in fact, quite striking. But the interesting phenomenon here is that these stories are transmitted on television along with all the other programs. Obviously the programmers at the television stations expect that people by themselves are able to judge between truth, fiction, and fantasy in the reports and fanciful psychotherapeutic theories. But are they really able to differentiate? There seems to have appeared a whole faction, which is very difficult to assess by ordinary means.

I maintain that the modern fantasy story—*The Lord of the Rings* being the masterpiece—precisely because it is fantasy is capable of wielding all such themes, including their mythological and religious aspects. For some time now, it is likely that more children in Western societies have learned about good and evil and how a decent person behaves from *The Lord of the Rings* rather than from the Bible. Modern fantasy stories were probably unthinkable outside a Judeo-Christian cultural background, but their dialogue with religious issues is normally hidden in the fantasy universe itself. I suggest we look into some of these modern eschatological stories to try to understand a little more about what is being compensated for.

I shall begin with the novel called *Momo,* written by the German author Michael Ende. The story takes place in a poor suburban Italian city. In the ruins of an old Roman amphitheater, literally in the wreckage of classical Western culture, lives a young orphan girl. This is Momo, and she has a special gift. She is able to listen to anybody so that he or she feels responded to and becomes able to reciprocate. So all the poor people nearby bring her food and clothes and the children visit her to play in the ruins, and never have they played so wonderfully as when they are near Momo. The people are poor, but they live in a warm community with each other.

Then evil creeps in. Evil is incarnated by a number of odd grey gentlemen in city dress, always smoking small, grey cigars. They go around, explaining that they represent the time bank, and they make people agree to save their time and put all their saved time in the grey men's bank. Strangely enough, the grey men are immediately forgotten once the contract has been made. The contract is real enough, however, a fact proven by the effect: everybody is becoming more and more stressed and hunted. Nobody has time for anything other than the pursuit of time and money. Momo receives fewer and fewer visits. The community decays. One day, a grey gentleman visits Momo and offers her a fine mechanical doll that speaks. But Momo's gift of listening to the true voice in anyone makes her immune to the seduction. The grey men set out to destroy her, but Momo receives help from a strange turtle who leads her to Master Hora, a name meaning "Lord of the Hour," that is, the time.

"Are you Death?" asks Momo. But Master Hora answers that if men really knew death they would not fear it. And if they did not fear death, nobody could steal their living time.

Master Hora takes Momo into a chamber at the heart of time, a cosmic, golden place where a giant pendulum slowly swings. By its movement flowers grow and wither away. These flowers are what the time robbers want; they are the living time that belongs to every person.

The time robbers—the grey gentlemen—keep the flowers in bank boxes, and they maintain themselves by smoking the leaves of the flowers. Without these cigars, the time robbers vanish like smoke. Master Hora's trick is to stop all time in the world, except for a single one-hour time flower, which he gives to Momo. In this one hour, she must see to it that all the time robbers disappear, and she must also liberate the time flowers from the bank so that they will be returned to their people. If she fails in the attempt, all the world will remain frozen forever. But she succeeds, of course, and she is a heroine because of her special gift of being able to listen to the true voice in anybody. The true voice of the grey men is the voice of the void, of emptiness.

In a novel by the Danish author Hanne Marie Svendsen, *The Gold Ball*, we find a number of similarly odd gentlemen. This novel is inspired by the prophecy of the Vølve, which I mentioned earlier. The novel takes place on an indeterminate Danish island in a family in which the golden globe passes from one woman to another. The golden globe has a typical magical quality in that its keeper does not become older.

We follow birth, life, and death, generation follows generation, individuals appear and pass away, and they all live in and by nature. But then evil creeps in. Beings become things, and nature slowly declines.

The odd men in city dress, called the gentlemen Hokbien, again represent evil. They talk about economics, mortgages, debts, and payments, and they always carry briefcases. They are difficult to tell apart. Once, two of them invaded the workshop of the blacksmith, and he cast them into the sea: "Begone," said the blacksmith. "They will make it, if they are meant to." The next day, a black coat is found on the beach along with many small wheels connected by ingenious mechanisms. The blacksmith does some serious thinking, as he has always had a hunch that there was something strange about the gentlemen Hokbien. A month later, the family receives a letter from Mr. Hokbien, as though nothing has happened. He is at their service as always. The gentlemen Hokbien are without mortal flesh. One is always interchangeable with another. Although they seem a bit ridiculous, the forces behind them are inevitable and fearsome.

In traditional fairy tales, one often meets the idea that the devil has power to give gold and riches in return for one's soul. He gives something material in return for something immaterial and spiritual. But after centuries of industrialization and, more recently, digitization, something really weird has happened that has changed the old deal: gold has become money, and money has become numbers, electronically transferred from one account to another. We now have something without weight or substance that nevertheless controls everything, which was more or less how one defined spirit in ancient times. Everything has been turned upside down: the old-fashioned spiritual has now become demonic. Compare this with the world of the old gods, where the world suffered from too much physical nature and primitive affects. But now the opposite condition is described: the present-day demons are totally without feelings and passions, without flesh and blood, without nature. In *The Lord of the Rings*, Sauron is without a real body; Treebeard says about Saruman that he "has a mind of metal and wheels; and he does not care for growing things" (2:76).

The gentlemen Hokbien and the time robbers seem perhaps like simple allegories of the stress, rush, and mechanical way of living everybody complains about. But are they really so simple? Let us look a bit closer.

It is noteworthy that the modern demon, the present evil, is no longer presented as a power of chaos, as it always used to be. On the contrary, the grey men incarnate a perfect order, a complete totality, which, however, swallows all individuality, all living life, and all disorderly nature. But it is an order of emptiness; this kind of order takes the meaning and purpose out of any individual's life and dissolves the mutual bonds in the community.

Such a phenomenon is the enemy in another of Michael Ende's books, probably his most well-known, *The Neverending Story*. The imperial country Fantastica faces a terrible and fearsome threat, called the nothingness. The nothingness spreads. Oddly enough, although the nothingness is terrifying, it nonetheless has a peculiar gravitational force. All are unavoidably drawn into it if they get too close. We are told that beings from Fantastica, who disappear into the nothingness, reappear in the human world in the form of lies. The hero—a fat, clumsy, unhappy, motherless boy named Bastian—is reading about it all in a book. He becomes part of the story within a story as he is the only one who knows the problem: the empress needs a new name. Only after his arrival into the new story does he slowly realize that the problem is only half solved, but that part must rest here.

My next example is Ursula Le Guin's story, *The Earthsea Trilogy*. It takes place in a completely magical universe where other laws exist than on our earth. The hero is Ged, who begins his career as a lonely, proud, and ambitious boy but ends up a dragonlord and Archmage. As Archmage, that is, the top wizard of the civilized world, he is summoned, in volume three, when something is threatening the whole cosmos. Again the danger is a mysterious contagious phenomenon, which is possessing people everywhere. The magic is disappearing from the world; the wizards are forgetting their spells. The cause is a powerful wizard who is promising eternal life to people in return for their true names. And—as anybody knows—the name is a decisive thing in a magical universe. The central art of the mages is to know the true names of all kinds of beings. When the true name is spoken in a spell, the object of the spell will be created, transformed, or destroyed. Anything of which one knows the true name is in one's power.

So when people give away their true names to the seducer to avoid death, they give away their essence of being. No wonder the meaning of life disappears at the same time. And what's more: the art of the mages withers away. Nobody believes in the word of creation anymore. Everything becomes empty and void.

Ged's last great battle takes place in "the dry land," the kingdom of death, a place of shadows like the Greek Hades. Ged fights the seducer, who turns out to be a wizard, long dead himself and yet undead, a spiritual vampire living through others' lives because he was a man who feared death more than anything. Ged wins the fight, and the world is restored. But so difficult is the battle that all of his magic power is spent. He returns to his native island and has to learn to live like an ordinary man, with a woman, but that is the story that continues beyond the trilogy.

One last example I shall take from Franz Werfel. His book, *Star of the Unborn* (1946), takes place in a distant future into which the hero is taken. He has been evoked as a curious wedding present for a young couple, and now he is being guided around this strange world. It is a world that looks like a paradise. Everything is good, everybody has enough, and death seems to have been overcome. When a person has had his or her fill of days and years, he or she goes voluntarily to the Winter Garden to be transformed into a flower. But gradually, the hero realizes that something is very, very wrong. In the end, there is a violent fight between the culture people and what are called the jungle people. The building that is the absolute center of the community and contains all science and culture is burning. Both sides know that this is an absolute tragedy. In the building is the Isokranium. It is not clear to the characters what this really is, but it is the most important item in this world and it has a deep spiritual significance. Without it, everything will go to pieces. A young Star Dancer volunteers to rescue the Isokranium and comes back, burned all over and deeply in pain. He is dying. Helpers want to soothe his pain and bring him to the Winter Garden, but the young man refuses. The possibility of redemption comes about through this choice of suffering and death. Through this choice, he brings back natural death, and he gives new life to all his people

Again and again, we see in modern eschatological stories two paramount factors: the terror of time and of death. The stories seem to insist that when we want to get rid of death in time, the result will be dead time, emptiness, and meaninglessness. Then life itself becomes a kingdom of shadows.

In all the stories I have mentioned, with the exception of *The Gold Ball* (where the problem is avoided), one single individual—or hobbit—has to confront the powers of unlife in the decisive situation. Unlike the stories of earlier times, this individual is neither the heroic man who is firm in faith and hope nor the tragic hero who is led by fate in an unavoidable way.

It is, in fact, striking how often there is a long and difficult phase near the end, during which the hero is totally convinced that what he or she does is of absolutely no use. The superiority of the forces against them is too great, and they themselves are much too small and powerless. This is clear: both hope and faith are long gone. But still the hero goes on. Why? Because there is absolutely nothing else left to do other than to go through with the journey into and through the emptiness and nothingness, the dry land. They know this is the only way to restore life among people, and this has become more important to them than their own lives. The stories insist that this fight, seemingly so impossible, after all is the only possible way, that individual decency and compassion are the decisive thing for the future of the world.

13   ANTHROPOS: THE COSMIC MAN

About 40,000 years ago or even more, homo sapiens had become what we human beings basically still are. Around that time, the use of fireplaces became common, decorated tools were shaped, and the wonderful cave paintings in Europe and Africa were created (Skogemann 1986, p. 86). These paintings are the oldest testimony to date of a human psyche so developed that images could be created from their inner representations in the painters. Our ancestors of course knew the animals intimately—but the animals were not present at the time the paintings were made. Furthermore, although we shall never know precisely what the paintings meant, it is certain that they meant *something* far beyond aesthetic expressions.

This implies that a symbolic dimension of the mind had become present. The ability to symbolize is so natural for us that we don't think about the quantum leap in consciousness it shows. The human psyche began to project itself onto symbolic images of the world: the animals, the natural landscapes, the sun, moon, and stars, gods and the beyond—the birth of archetypal images as it were.

Many mythologies contain an image of a "first" being of cosmic dimensions from whom the world comes into being. In Indian mythology, his name was Yama or, in the Upanishads, Purusha, an androgynous figure whose name means "human"; when he was sacrificed by the gods, the four castes arose from his limbs, and the rest of the universe from his other parts. In China, P'an Ku shaped the universe, and when he died, the five holy mountains in China originated from his limbs and trunk and from his eyes came the sun and the moon. In Jewish mythology, Adam was sometimes a cosmic, androgynous giant. In ancient Persia, Gayōmart was murdered by the evil Ahriman, but the eight metals flew from his body and from his semen sprouted rhubarb stalks from which the first human couple originated. In Norse mythology, it was the giant Ymir: of his flesh the earth was shaped, of his bones the mountains, and of his scull the heavens, and from him the gods originated, and when they grew in strength they gathered and slew Ymir.

All of these are ancient sacrificial myths that read like the program of a ritual drama; a symbolic creation ceremony implicit in the cutting up of the sacrificial victim and its preparation for being cooked. In his essay on ritual drama, W. Grønbech (1931) explains in depth how the persons acting in such rituals actually became the gods, that is, the clan personified. As the original sacrifice was repeated, the cosmos was created out of a vague grayness and so was the life of the clan—which we would call the group self. In Grønbech's opinion, the actions of the drama were executed prior in time to the mythological explanation of what was going on in the ritual. This is similar to Jung's hypothesis that all the psychic functions which we today think of as conscious, once were unconscious but nevertheless functioned as though they were conscious, that is, they were following a purely archetypal pattern (Jung 1954c, par. 412).

On a fundamental level, we still build all our mental representations of our surroundings through projections. The human psychic system is organized and structured through the cultural processes that decide the ways and means by which our human needs can be satisfied. This is for the psyche what the ecosystem is for the living organism. In growing up, we take in a whole world along with our mothers' milk which fills the matrix of the inborn archetypal system. Even though such worlds are not hermetically sealed between the various human cultures, it is still a special achievement to transcend great cultural differences, something that people in exile know involuntarily and anthropologists reflect upon professionally.

Jung wrote:

> The symbols of the circle and the quaternity, the hallmarks of the individuation process, point back, on the one hand, to the original and primitive order of human society, and forward on the other to an inner order of the psyche. It is as though the psyche were the indispensable instrument in the reorganizing of a civilized community. (1946, par. 539)

Taken literally, the circle and quaternity in tribal and ancient societies are the architectonic basic forms used for city walls, temples, and castles, structures built to defend people and values. They have their counterparts in the healthy defenses of the self of the individual: first is the capacity to symbolize; this is the precondition for natural creativity. Second is the capacity of the self to organize the interplay between the outer and inner worlds. The healthy self has the capacity to interrelate in a creative way with those symbolic, emotional, and ideational structures in its surroundings that can support the basic needs of the personality for identity and meaning. I am not referring to a primitive or infantile identity here, but rather the basic interplay with the world in which we live. We never outgrow that, it just changes form.

The Anthropos symbol became important in another way in alchemy in the Middle Ages. From his workings with the material components, the alchemist strived to put together the Anthropos, the spirit hiding in matter. Jung became a collector of and an expert in alchemical scripts. He found in alchemy a forerunner of his own psychology.

As a professor of the English of the Middle Ages, Tolkien, too, must have read alchemical texts. In his essays he refers to alchemy a number of times. Discussing "Sir Gawain and the Green Knight," he says that fairy-stories can do something that a realistic story cannot:

> It is one of the properties of Fairy-Story thus to
> enlarge the scene and the actors; or rather it is one of
> the properties that are *distilled by literary alchemy* when
> old deep-rooted stories are rehandled by a real poet
> with an imagination of his own. (Tolkien 1983, p.
> 125; italics added)

I wonder whether he would have written that in 1953 without having himself and *The Lord of The Rings*, which was published the next year after fourteen years of work, in mind!

Jung realized that the making of gold and elixirs of immortality were not the true goals of alchemy; he saw alchemy as a psychological process establishing a relation to the self. Tolkien, too, differentiated between the outer and inner aspects of alchemy. The outer aspect absolutely did not have Tolkien's sympathy. This becomes clear in the story about Gondor's past that Faramir tells Frodo and Sam:

> "Death was ever present, because the Númenoreans still, as they had in their old kingdom, and so lost it, hungered after endless life unchanging. Kings made tombs more splendid than houses of the living, and counted old names in the rolls of their descent dearer than the names of sons. Childless lords sat in aged halls musing on heraldry; in secret chambers withered men compounded strong elixirs, or in high cold towers asked questions of the stars." (2:286)

Tolkien created a whole fictional universe. The building blocks, of course, are his enormous knowledge of languages, mythology, legends, fairy tales, and ancient poetry. But as he broke down the original buildings and reused the "blocks" in new ways, and then distilled the material year after year, unavoidable, numinous archetypal symbols appeared—just as they did to the alchemists.

Jung thought that the archetypal images had their source in the collective unconscious. In analytical practice, therefore, the Jungian analyst should know a lot about mythology, fairy tales, and the history of symbols to be aware of such symbols appearing in the dreams and fantasies of the patient, and possibly to amplify them to bring life into them through the connection to a context larger than the purely personal.

By comparison, as the author of *The Lord of the Rings*, Tolkien has the role of the analyst in relation to his readers. The important thing is not his sources, but the alchemical or therapeutic effect on the reader. According to Tolkien, a good fairy-story can bring consolation and healing to its time. He believed that fairy tales always, that is, since the beginnings of language, have been boiling in the "Pot of Soup," the "Cauldron of Story," and new bits have been continually added to it by individual storytellers (1983, p. 125). The highest form of fairy-story is the eucatastrophic tale, which has a very powerful, numinous effect:

> In such stories when the sudden turn [the eucatastrophe] comes we get a piercing glimpse of joy, and heart's desire, that for a moment passes outside the frame, rends indeed the very web of story, and lets a gleam come through. (ibid., p. 154)

The Lord of the Rings has many such moments where the reader is simultaneously carried away, delighted, and blinded by tears, thanks to Tolkien's literary alchemy.

The archetype of the Anthropos in analytical psychology forms the basis of our humanity, our social being. Of the Self as a group, Jung writes:

> As a matter of fact a positive relationship between the individual and society or a group is essential, since no individual stands by himself but depends upon symbiosis with a group. The self, the very centre of

an individual, is of a conglomerate nature. It is, as it were, a group. It is a collectivity in itself and therefore always, when it works most positively, creates a group. (1973, vol. 1, p. 508)

The challenge of the Ring in the story is countered through another kind of development. The problem the Ring presents forces the members of the Fellowship to form an individuating collective by means of an emerging unbreakable friendship that within itself unites opposites, small with big, mortal with immortal, elf with dwarf. One very central feature of *The Lord of the Rings* is that it shows the reader so many aspects of individuation in a complex and moving way.

On the unconscious or natural level, the archetype manifests itself in the tribal community, as described above, through rituals and traditions. The Anthropos is connected with the number four. According to Jung, the quaternity indicates the possibility of becoming conscious.

Anthropos symbolizes the whole man, just as the new age, Aquarius, does in our ordinary world if one listens to the speculations of astrologers on the meaning of the image of the "water-bearer."

On the conscious level, Tolkien makes use of the numbers that are considered holy in the Judeo-Christian tradition. These appear, from the motto of *The Lord of the Rings*, to be 1, 3, 7, and 9. But looking closer, a lot of elements are really based on four and the multiplicity of four. I have throughout this book mentioned a number of them, such as the four rivers, the four forests, and the typical mandala structures of the cities.

Elrond declares that the Fellowship must have nine members equaling the nine Ringwraiths. Boromir is appointed as one of the Company, but he never takes part in the same spirit as the others and he dies early in the story. I think that the real Fellowship consists of the eight individuals we follow all the way through and who are united again in Minas Tirith, if only for a short time, near the end. Psychologically, it is meaningful to count the Fellowship as two times four. The first quaternity consists of the four hobbits representing the Ego archetype and the second quaternity consists of spirit, man, elf, and dwarf, a temporary representation of the Self. Legolas and Gimli transcend the old hostility between elves and dwarves, or as one might say, an opposition between the ethereal and the subterranean.

The two quaternities also form a correspondence between the conscious world and the archetypal world. Frodo corresponds to Gandalf, Sam to Aragorn, and the friends Merry and Pippin correspond to Gimli and Legolas.

The first contact between the small world and the big world takes place between Frodo and Gandalf. During the whole journey from Moria to Mordor, Frodo believes that Gandalf is dead, but Gandalf still functions as an inner guide to Frodo. Where Gandalf humiliated Saruman in Orthanc, Frodo repeats the same humiliation on a smaller scale in the Shire without knowing it. For both of them, life in Middle-earth is over when their task has been done.

Sam corresponds to Aragorn. As I discussed earlier, Sam follows the typical hero pattern of the fairy tale, while Aragorn follows the mythological hero pattern. Both become masters where before they were servants; Aragorn becomes king, and Sam becomes the mayor of the Shire. The one rules for one hundred and twenty years, the other for sixty. Both Aragorn and Sam are motivated by love, and both of them win their brides.

So the Fellowship begins as two purely male quaternities and ends up as two quaternities each with three males and one female, just like the typical fairy-tale pattern I have referred to earlier. The feminine and love were lacking but have by the end taken their symbolic places. To complete the fourness symbols, we pass from the Third to the Fourth Age, the Age of Man.

After the new kingdom has been established, King Aragorn declares that no Big People may cross the borders of the Shire. On the other hand, the hobbits can go anywhere they like. In a psychological interpretation, this means that there is established a new balance between the ego and the unconscious. The original narrowness of the consciousness has disappeared, and so has the risk of being overwhelmed by archetypal powers from the collective unconscious, as they are now forbidden to enter.

The conscious ego has established a firm relation to the self and thereby has access to the archetypal world as a creative resource. Aragorn has become the personification of the Self. He personifies the "Green Man," the bringer of hope and healing. In the Arabic alchemical tradition, the Green Man is *El-Khidr*, who finds the spring of life. Jung compares him with the *lapis*, the stone of the wise in the European alchemical tradition. England had its own traditional Green Man, who is connected to death and rebirth and known from pictures and legends. Tolkien himself translated and commented on one of the oldest epic poems, "Sir Gawain and the Green Knight," where the Green Knight is a mysterious figure who forces Gawain to go on a quest.

In *The Lord of the Rings*, Aragorn first appears strange-looking and weather-beaten, wrapped in a dark-green cloak and mud-caked boots. Although a Green Man from the very beginning, he has not yet taken the exalted form that he has in the end. As a king, he takes his name after the shining green gem, the elfstone, thereby symbolically comprising the Green Man of fairy tales and the alchemical *lapis*. At the departure of the hobbits, Aragorn is described as an almost divine figure:

> With that they parted, and it was then the time
> of sunset; and when after a while they turned and
> looked back, they saw the King of the West sitting
> upon his horse with his knights about him; and the
> falling Sun shone upon them and made all their
> harness to gleam like red gold, and the white mantle
> of Aragorn was turned to a flame. Then Aragorn took
> the green stone and held it up, and there came a green
> fire from his hand. (3:260)

14 THE RENEWAL
OF THE
SHIRE

Although the journey back to the Shire takes half a year, it is not because the hobbits meet the great hardships of the journey out. They more or less follow in the footsteps of their previous route—through the forest of Drùadan, on to Edoras where the body of King Théoden is buried, then to Helm's Deep because of Legolas's promise to visit the Glittering Caves. After that, the travelers go to Isengard, where Legolas and Gimli say goodbye to the rest and set off to wander in Fangorn together. In Rohan, Aragorn leaves them, and close to the gates of Moria it is Celeborn and Galadriel who part from the hobbits. They reach Rivendell on Bilbo's birthday and spend a couple of weeks there together with Gandalf. Finally, Gandalf too breaks off to talk to Tom Bombadil after a short visit at the Prancing Pony in Bree.

> "Well here we are, just the four of us that started out together," said Merry. "We have left all the rest behind, one after another. It seems almost like a dream that has slowly faded."
>
> "Not to me," said Frodo. "To me it feels more like falling asleep again." (3:276)

I have interpreted the quest as a collective individuation, a confrontation with the collective unconscious and its archetypes. The ego in the shape of the four hobbits has become transformed and expanded through this confrontation. Now it appears that the change has been most necessary and will serve the essential goal: to renew the Shire.

The Shire seemed to need "an invasion of dragons" long before Frodo set off; in the meantime the Shire certainly has been invaded by nasty influences, but the hobbits have, in Gandalf's words, "been trained" to settle its affairs themselves (3:275).

Suddenly, it seems as if the previous thousand-some pages were only an intermezzo before the real task, which was unfinished business going back as far as the time of Bilbo's journey. Bilbo made his journey as a typical smug hobbit, and he returned as an eccentric in *The Hobbit*; that heritage he passed on to Frodo. Neither changed anything about the Shire. Frodo would have liked to experience some private adventures like Bilbo, but each time he thought with the one half of his consciousness that now he would go, the other half of his consciousness cried: "Not yet" (1:52). Such is the attitude of the average person. One ought to do this and that, but one just doesn't. One does not really adapt to one's inner and outer circumstances, not unless or until a crisis of some sort forces one to change one's life completely. And in the meantime, the problem grows.

During the one year Frodo and the other hobbits have been away, the Shire has been transformed into a miniature version of Isengard, which itself was a toy model of Barad-dûr.

The Shire has become a recognizable version of everything a Western, freedom-loving, democratic person should not put up with. So now at the end of the story we have some instruction in the workings of civil courage with the aim of fighting suppression. We have left the grand archetypal or magic world. In the Shire, there is just ordinary cowardice, greediness, envy, and grudges, ordinary avarice of power, social suppression, and neglect of both community and nature. The kind of thing that can happen anywhere if one is not careful.

Sam, Merry, and Pippin feel "the great dream" disappear while they themselves wake up; Frodo, on the other hand, has disappeared into that dream, and he cannot adapt to everyday life again.

When the hobbits return to the Shire, Merry and Pippin, who began as carefree young boys, take their place as the obvious leaders in the revolution against the totalitarian forces that have taken over their country. In the beginning, they try to laugh it off, but when one of the rascals begins to insult Frodo, it is too much for Pippin:

> His thoughts went back to the Field of Cormallen, and here was a squint-eyed rascal calling the Ring-bearer "little cock-a-whoop." He cast back his cloak, flashed out his sword, and the silver and sable of Gondor gleamed on him as he rode forward.
>
> "I am a messenger of the King," he said. "You are speaking to the King's friend, and one of the most renowned in all the lands of the West. You are a ruffian and a fool. Down on your knees in the road

and ask pardon, or I will set this troll's bane in you!"
(3:284–85)

The rascals flee, but Pippin and Merry realize that they have
had only a postponement of a confrontation. The villains
will return with reinforcements. Frodo, for his part, is shaken
and sad, but he does not want to think of fight and killing.
Sam suggests, probably with a certain Rose in mind, that
they seek refuge with Tom Cotton and his numerous sons.
Merry conceives of a more far-reaching plan; they have to
wake up the Shire immediately:

> "They hate all this, you can see: all of them except
> perhaps one or two rascals, and a few fools that
> want to be important, but don't at all understand
> what is really going on. But Shire-folk have been so
> comfortable so long they don't know what to do.
> They just want a match, though, and they'll go up
> in fire." (3:286)

All end up in the great Battle of Bywater where the
hobbits come out victorious. There are seventy dead enemies
and a dozen prisoners, but also nineteen hobbits have fallen.
Because this has been the only big battle in the history of
the hobbits for several hundred years, much is written about
it in the annals of the Shire. And most of all, Pippin and
Merry have won a great reputation among people.

> "Lordly" folk called them, meaning nothing but good;
> for it warmed all hearts to see them go riding by
> with their mail-shirts so bright and their shields so
> splendid, laughing and singing songs of far away; and

if they were now large and magnificent, they were unchanged otherwise, unless they were indeed more fairspoken and more jovial and full of merriment than ever before. (3:305)

At the age of forty-six, Merry "The Magnificent" becomes Master of Buckland, and two years later at the age of forty-two, Pippin, not surprisingly, becomes the Took and Thain for the Shire. Thirty years later, his oldest son, Faramir, marries Sam's second daughter, Goldilocks. Nothing is told about the marriage of Merry, although it is said that when he was 102 years old, he passed his office to his son and traveled with Pippin to Gondor where they stayed with Aragorn until they died.

Sam's part is wholly different. He is the gardener with the really green thumbs, a small Green Man. He is deeply shaken by the destruction of the living nature in the Shire. The trees have been cut down, including the tree in the middle of the Party Field where Bilbo held his speech. It lies lopped off and dead, similar to the old white tree in Gondor. The party tree is a symbol like the Tree of Life to the people of the Shire.

When all the fighting is over, Sam remembers the gift of Galadriel. Sam feels sure that it is not only for himself but must be used for the good of all hobbits (3:303). He plants lots of new trees and puts a single grain of dust from Galadriel's box with each sapling. At last he goes to the Three-Farthing Stone in the center of the Party Field and casts the remaining dust in the air with a blessing. And finally he places the small silver nut where the party tree stood. The whole winter he waits impatiently.

Spring and summer surpass all years in fertility. Sam marries his Rose. The trees grow as if one year made up for twenty (3:303). On the Party Field, a *mallorn* tree with golden flowers sprouts from the silver nut. Eventually, it becomes very beautiful and famous, the only *mallorn* tree west of the mountains and east of the sea. All the children born in the Shire in this year, 1420, are healthy and beautiful and many have golden hair, which used to be very rare with the hobbits. The golden queen has obviously set her stamp. Sam's own firstborn daughter, Elanor, is golden haired and very beautiful, too. For Sam, Merry, and Pippin life flourishes in all aspects.

But sadly, it is not so for Frodo. Quietly he withdraws from life without the rightful recognition he deserves for his great deed (3:305). Sam sees this and is pained by it.

The next year, Frodo asks Sam to follow him. They go to the Grey Havens, as Sam could well guess they would, to see Bilbo one last time. But only when they are there does Sam realize that Frodo is leaving him and going with Bilbo, Galadriel, Elrond, Gandalf, and Cirdan. Frodo says to Sam that he can't come with them:

> "Though you too were a Ring-bearer, if only for a little while. Your time may come. Do not be too sad, Sam. You cannot be always torn in two. You will have to be one and whole, for many years. You have so much to enjoy and to be, and to do."
>
> "But," said Sam, and tears started in his eyes, "I thought you were going to enjoy the Shire, too, for years and years, after all you have done."

"So I thought too, once. But I have been too deeply hurt, Sam. I tried to save the Shire, and it has been saved, but not for me. It must often be so, Sam, when things are in danger: some one has to give them up, lose them, so that others may keep them. But you are my heir: all that I had and might have had I leave to you." (3:309)

And Sam is the one who is granted the last words of the story:

But Sam turned to Bywater, and so came back up the Hill, as day was ending once more. And he went on, and there was yellow light, and fire within; and the evening meal was ready, and he was expected. And Rose drew him in, and set him in his chair, and put little Elanor upon his lap.
He drew a deep breath. "Well, I'm back," he said. (3:311)

Sam really has a long and rich life; he and Rose have thirteen children together; seven times he is elected as mayor in the Shire, and at the end of his last term he is ninety-six years old. Six years later, Rose dies, and it is told in the appendix that Sam then goes to the Grey Havens and sails over the sea to Valinor as the last of the Ring-bearers.

In the *Silmarillion* and in *The Lord of the Rings*, mortality versus immortality plays an enormous part on all levels. Tolkien works hard to make his good characters accept death, as Aragorn does with great dignity in contrast to his grandiose ancestors from Númenor who strived to win immortality from Valinor and perished in a flood. Frodo, for his part, is offered only a temporary stay by Arwen:

> "But in my stead you shall go, Ring-bearer, when the time comes, and if you then desire it. If your hurts grieve you still and the memory of your burden is heavy, then you may pass into the West, until all your wounds and weariness are healed." (3:252–53)

Bilbo, who is also boarding the ship, says that now when he has become the oldest hobbit ever, it is all right to go on the last journey—a classical metaphor for death. Sam, however, is not a sufferer. He has not been wounded by wearing the Ring. He returned home to a long and happy life and flourishing psychic health. The gardner Sam makes everything grow and thrive, blessed by Galadriel. He ought to die satisfied with his years.

Tolkien writes, in his essay "On Fairy-Stories," that the oldest and deepest desire in humans, which is satisfied by fairy-stories, is that they tell about the great escape: escape from death (1983, p. 153). So finally, well hidden in the appendix, Tolkien forgets all his official ethics and satisfies this desire on behalf of the reader: Sam is rewarded with unconditional access to the Island of the Immortals.

NOTES

1. Tolkien's own title for this lecture was "A Hobby for the Home" (Tolkien 1983, p. 3).

2. See Tolkien, "Valedictory Address" (1959), in *"The Monsters and the Critics"* (1983, p. 226): "But I am, as I say, an amateur. And if that means that I have neglected parts of my large field, devoting myself to those things that I personally like, it does also mean that I have tried to awake liking, to communicate delight in those things that I find enjoyable."

3. For an online bibliography of works on this subject, visit http://www.baltes-paul.de/Wisdom.html

4. The church father Augustine: *Non est ergo malum nisi privatio boni.* This is said against the Manichean heresy, which holds a dualistic worldview with an evil power opposed to a good god.

5. Boëthius was a Christian Roman senator who was tortured to death in 524 A.D. In prison, he wrote *De Consolatione Philosophiae*, in which he, like Augustine, claimed that evil does not exist and cannot create. What we think is evil (for example, to be executed) is in reality, on a divine level, good. The Manicheans were dualists and saw the world as a battlefield between good and evil.

LITERATURE

Blixen, Karen (Isak Dinesen). 1934. *Seven Gothic Tales*. New York: Harrison Smith and Robert Haas.

Carpenter, Humphrey, and Tolkien, C., eds. 1981. *Letters of J. R. R. Tolkien*. London: Allen & Unwin.

Conrad, Joseph. 1902. *Heart of Darkness/Congo Diary and Upriver Book*. London: Hesperus, 2002.

Cunninghame Graham, R. B. 1928. "Higginson's Dream." In *Thirteen Stories*. London: Duckworth.

Ende, Michael. 1974. *Momo*. London: Puffin Books.

———. 1983. *The Neverending Story*. London: Puffin Books.

Grønbech, W. 1931. Essay on ritual drama. In *Culture of the Teutons*, vol. 2. London: Jespersen og Pios forlag.

Hansen, J. V. 1996. *Englene—og al deres væsen*. Copenhagen: Gyldendal.

Hynes, William J., and Doty, William G., eds. 1993. *Mythical Trickster Figures: Contours, Contexts, and Criticism*. Tuscaloosa: University of Alabama Press.

Jung, C. G. 1942. Paracelsus as a spiritual phenomenon. In *Collected Works*, vol. 13. Princeton, N.J.: Princeton University Press, 1967.

———. 1946. The psychology of the transference. In *Collected Works*, vol. 16. Princeton, N.J.: Princeton University Press, 1966.

———. 1948. On the phenomenology of the spirit in fairytales. In *Collected Works*, vol. 9i. Princeton, N.J.: Princeton University Press, 1968.

———. 1951. *Aion*. *Collected Works*, vol. 9ii. Princeton, N.J.: Princeton University Press, 1959.

———. 1952. Answer to Job. In *Collected Works*, vol. 11. Princeton, N.J.: Princeton University Press, 1969.

———. 1954a. Archetypes of the collective unconscious. In *Collected Works*, vol. 9i. Princeton, N.J.: Princeton University Press, 1968.

———. 1954b. On the psychology of the trickster figure. In *Collected Works*, vol. 9i. Princeton, N.J.: Princeton University Press, 1968.

———. 1954c. On the nature of the psyche. In *Collected Works*, vol. 8. Princeton, N.J.: Princeton University Press, 1969.

———. 1955–56. *Mysterium Coniunctionis. Collected Works*, vol. 14. Princeton, N.J.: Princeton University Press, 1970.

———. 1957. The undiscovered self (present and future). In *Collected Works*, vol. 10. Princeton, N.J.: Princeton University Press, 1964.

———. 1961a. Symbols and the interpretation of dreams. In *Collected Works*, vol. 18. Princeton, N.J.: Princeton University Press, 1976.

———. 1961b. *Memories, Dreams, Reflections.* New York: Pantheon Books, 1973.

———. 1972. *Man and His Symbols.* London: Aldus.

———. 1973. *Letters*, vols. 1 and 2. Princeton, N.J.: Princeton University Press.

Kalched, D. E. 1996. *The Inner World of Trauma: Archetypal Defenses of the Personal Spirit.* London: Routledge.

Le Guin, Ursula K. 1968. *A Wizard of Earthsea.* New York: Atheneum.

———. 1971. *The Tombs of Atuan.* New York: Atheneum.

———. 1972. *The Farthest Shore.* New York: Atheneum.

Lindqvist, Sven. 1996. *Exterminate All the Brutes.* New York: The New Press.

O'Neill, Timothy. 1979. *The Individuated Hobbit.* Boston: Houghton Miffin Company.

Ott, Nancy Marie. 2002. J. R. R. Tolkien and World War II. Retrieved on February 24, 2009, at http://greenbooks.theonering.net/guest/files/040102_02.html

Shippey, Tom. 2000. *J. R. R. Tolkien: Author of the Century*. London: HarperCollins Publishers.

Skogemann, Pia. 1986. *Arketyper*. Copenhagen: Lindhardt og Ringhof.

———. 1990. Selvets mørke nat. In *C. G. Jung, Nazisme og psychology*, Sv.Aa. Madsen, P. Skogemann, and S. Visholm, eds. Copenhagen: Politisk Revy.

———. 1992. *Er jeg en sommerfugl, der drømmer?* Copenhagen: Lindhardt og Ringhof.

Skogemann, P., ed. 2001. *En karl var min mor, en fisk*. Copenhagen: Lindhardt og Ringhof.

Striderzo, Enzo. 2003. *The Origins of Nazi Violence*. New York: The New Press.

Svendsen, Hanne Marie. 1989. *The Gold Ball*. Jorgen Schiott, trans. New York: Knopf.

Tjalve, Lars. 2002. *Ringenes Herre og den bibelske fortælling*. Copenhagen: Forlaget Unitas.

Tolkien, J. R. R. 1954, 1955. *The Lord of the Rings*, 3 vols., second edition. New York: Houghton Mifflin, 1988.

———. 1975. *Farmer Giles of Ham / The Adventures of Tom Bombadil*. London: Unwin Paperbacks.

———. 1983. *The Monsters and the Critics and Other Essays*. London: Allen & Unwin.

———. 1989. *The J. R. R. Tolkien Reader*. New York: Ballantine Books.

———. 1999. *Silmarillion*. London: HarperCollins.

von Franz, M.-L. 1997. *Archetypal Patterns in Fairy Tales*. Toronto: Inner City Books.

Wells, H. G. 1897. *The Invisible Man*. London: Penguin Books, 2005.

———. 1898. *War of the Worlds*. London: Penguin Books, 2005.

Werfel, Franz. 1946. *The Star of the Unborn*. New York: Viking Press.

West, L. Jolyon, and Martin, R. 1994. Pseudo-identity and the treatment of personality change in victims of captivity and cults. In *Dissociation: Clinical and Theoretical Perspectives*, S. J. Lynn and J. W. Rhue, eds. New York: The Guilford Press.

INDEX

active imagination, 2–3, 14
addiction, narcotic, 21
Ainulindalë, 153, 156
alchemy, xv, 148–49, 186–87, 191; literary, 186, 188
alien abduction, 174
anger, 132
anima/Anima, xiv, 103–6, 110; archetype, xvii; nature, 104
anima mundi, xiv
Anthropos, archetype, xvi, 62, 149, 188–89
Antichrist, 149
anti-Semitism, 158, 162
Aquarius, age of, 168, 189
archetypal images, x, 183, 187
archetypes, viii, x, 2, 151, 194; of transformation, xvii
art: as an expression of *Zeitgeist*, 6; modern, 7
Augustine, 158, 201n4–5

Baldr, 171–72
baptism, 173
Beowulf, xix–xx
Biano, Ochwiä, 158
Bible, 175
Blixen, Karen, 115
Boëthius, 156, 201n5
Bush, George W., 164

cages, fear of, 115
cave painting, 183
chaos, 154; versus order, 178–79
Christ, 149, 157
Christian dogma, 155, 157
Christianity, xx, 4, 156–59, 173; Jung's analysis in light of alchemical symbolism, 149
Clement, 157
clown, 77
colonialism, 158–59

Conrad, Joseph, 160–62
consciousness, xi, xiii, 11–14, 23, 34, 48, 77, 111, 183; alien form, 29; collective, 73, 123, 127, 149; historical, 20; human, 132; Sam's, 46; undifferentiated, 83
creation myth, Tolkien's, 153, 171
creativity, 186
Cunninghame Graham, R. B., 159

Dante, 106
Darwin, Charles, 159
dead, fear of, 66
death, 18–19, 29, 62–66, 69, 97, 101, 127, 129, 142, 163, 170–72, 176, 180–81, 199–200; and evil, 157; and rebirth, 62–63, 191; symbolic, 49; valley of, 32
demons, 171–72, 178
descent, 62–63, 66
Devil, 74, 178
dissociation, 166
dream-I, 165
dreams, ix, 7, 12, 59, 85, 89, 103, 129, 155, 165, 188

Earth, geological history, 154
ego/Ego, xi–xiii, 22, 45, 50, 85, 89, 147, 150, 164, 191, 194; archetypal, 10, 190
ego-consciousness, xii, 10, 12
elements, four classical, 64, 148–49
El-Khidr, 191
elven language. *See* languages, invented
Ende, Michael, 175, 179
English, Old or of the Middle Ages, xx, 15, 186
escapism, 2, 87
eschatology, 168–69
ethics, 164
eucatastrophe, 5, 188
evil, 7, 23, 62, 68, 74, 82, 147, 153, 156, 159, 164, 175, 177–78, 201n4–5;

evil (*continued*)
and death, 157; bringing about good,
33 (*see also* good and evil)
evolution, 159, 170

Faëry, 1
fairy tales, vii, ix, 1, 17, 29, 33–36, 43, 59,
103–4, 123, 129, 178, 187–88, 190, 192;
male pattern, xvi
fairy-stories (Tolkien's term), 1, 7, 14, 186,
188, 200
fantasies, ix, 1, 7, 85, 103, 165, 188;
mythological, 3, 172, 174; paranoid,
174; subconscious, viii
fantasy, literary format, 159, 168, 171, 175
fear, 66
feminine, 105, 111, 191
feminism, 113–14
fiction, eschatological, 168, 175, 181
filius macrocosmi, 149
fire, secret, 135
fool, 35, 38
forests, 58–62
Free Schools, xx
friendship, xvii, 25, 49, 127
Frodo, 15–34

Gayōmart, 184
gender role, masculine, 15
genocide, 157–59, 162
giants, 171–72
god, use of the word in *The Lord of the
Rings*, 126
goddesses, of wisdom, love, and war, 103
godlessness, 26
good and evil, 150, 154–56, 168, 175,
201n5
Grail, legends of, 1
grandiosity, 146–47
Green Knight, 192
Green Man, 191–92, 197
greenhouse effect, 172
Grimm brothers, 34
Grønbech, W., 184
Grundtvig, N. F. S., xix–xx, 169–70

hell, in the Middle Ages, 64, 69
Henderson, Joseph, 18, 85

heresy: Christian, 156; Manichean, 157,
201n4
Hermes, 55
hero/heroine, 17, 98; archetypal cultural,
86; archetype, 89, 95; mythological, 92,
100; of fairy tales versus mythological,
35, 43
hero myth, 85
hero pattern, 16, 190
Hitler, Adolf, 162
hobbits, 9–10, 13, 26, 52, 56, 72, 80, 84,
150, 154, 181, 191, 196, 198, 200; as an
ego-model, 14; etymology, 9
hobbit-consciousness, 15
højskoler (folk schools), xx
Holocaust, 158
Hussein, Saddam, 163

Ignatius Loyola, 29
Iliad, 132
immortality, 19, 32, 86–87, 126, 146, 187,
199–200
incest, 30
individuality, 178
individuation, xii–xiii, xv, 10, 15, 18, 23,
123, 134, 149–50, 185, 189; collective,
xvi, 194
inflation, 45, 147
initiation, 18, 23, 51
intuition, 14, 50–51
Iraqi war, 164
Islamism, 162

Jacob, and his dream about a ladder, 24
Jehovah's Witnesses, 167
Jesus, 169
Jung, C. G., 1–3, 5, 24, 67, 149, 184–87,
189; alchemy, 186–87, 191; *Answer
to Job*, 156–57; anima, 103; theory of
archetypes, vii; on art, 6–7; on demons,
171; problem of evil, 164; reaction
to Ochwiä Biano, 158–59; on spirit,
26–27, 133–34; synchronicity, 78;
trickster archetype, 83–84; typology, 14
Jungian lexicon, vii

kairos, xviii, 6
Kalched, Donald, 165

208

languages, invented (eg., elvish), 9, 67, 99
lapis philosophorum, 149, 191–92
Le Guin, Ursula, 179
life after death, 169–70
Lindqvist, Sven, 158–59, 162
love, 91, 98, 113–14, 117, 119, 124, 127, 150, 191
Lucas, George, ix
Lucifer, 154

magic, 1, 179
mandala, xviii, 2, 60–61, 74, 149, 189
Manichaeans, 156, 201n5
Mao, 163
Martin, R., 166
Marxism, 170
meaning, loss of, 26
Mercurius Duplex, xv, 129
Merry and Pippin, 48–54
Michael, the archangel, 139
Middle-earth, geography of, xvii, xix
mirror, as a metaphor for self-reflection, 23
mortality, 101 (*see also* immortality)
mother, evil, 30; negative archtype, 29, 43
Muhammad, 169
murder, 157
myths/mythology, vii, ix, 1, 43, 103–4, 187; biblical, 154; sacrificial, 184
mythology: Christian, 139; for England, xix; Indian, 184; invented, 67; Jewish, 184; Nordic, xix–xx; Norse, 184; Scandanavian, 171

natural sciences, 173
nature, 130, 173, 177–78
nature spirit, 83
Nazism, 157
night journey, 95

Odin, 171
Old King, archetype of, xiv, 123
O'Neill, Timothy, x, 147–48
Ott, Nancy Marie, 67

pacifism, 165
palantir, 13, 53, 73, 95, 140
P'an Ku, 184

paradise, dreams of, 169–70, 180
paranoia, 146
philosopher's stone, 149
pilgrimage, xviii, 18–19, 25
pollution, 74, 167, 172
possession, archetypal, 20
posttraumatic stress disorder (PTSD), 68, 87
power, 150, 160, 164
privatio boni, 155, 157
projection, 108, 172, 185
psyche: archetypal aspects, xiii; collective, 7; human, 183, 185; Jungian structural model, xi; male, xvi
psychosis, 3
psychotherapy, 5
Purusha, 184

quaternity, 185, 189–91

race, 159
rage, 154
Ragnarök, 171
rebirth, 20, 30, 49, 95 (*see also* death and rebirth)
redemption, 181
reincarnation, 170
religion, xx–xxi, 169
Ring, as a symbol, xiii
rites of passage, 49, 52
ritual drama, 184
rivers, crossing, 56–57
role-playing games, x

Saint George, 139
Saint Nicolas of Flüe, 24
Sam, 34–48
Satan, 139, 149, 157 (*see also* Devil)
Saxo Grammaticus, 113, 115
sea, associated with death, 72
self image, positive, 17
self/Self, 47, 58–61, 155, 165, 186–87, 190–91; archetype of, xiii, xviii, 38, 111, 147, 163; as a group, 184, 188; collective symbol, 149; dark side, 164; feminine aspect of, xvii; symbol of, 10, 62
self-care system, 165–66

self-knowledge, 5, 45, 61, 103
sensation, 51
serial killers, 165; in literature, 160
sexuality, in *The Lord of the Rings*, 104
shadow, xiv–xv, 5, 7, 31, 103, 163; collective
    and archetypal, 157–58; collective
    hobbit, 26; Frodo's, 23, 26, 31; of
    civilization, 160; of the white man, 162;
    personal, xv; Sam's, 47
Shippey, Tom, xix–xx, 13, 146, 150,
    155–56
Shire, the, xi–xiii, xviii
Silmarillion, 2, 7, 46, 80–81, 87, 101, 126,
    129–30, 150, 153–54, 171, 199
sin, 169, 172
song, magic, 59
Sophia, 110
spell, calling, 59
spirit, archetypal, 129, 131, 134
Stalin, 158
Stockholm syndrome, 166
Striderzo, Enzo, 158
Svendsen, Hanne Marie, 177
symbolize, ability to, 183, 186
symbols, 26; archetypal, viii, 187
synchronicity, 78
syzygy, 59, 61

terrorism, 162
The Hobbit, 9, 60, 194
The Red Book, 2
Thor, 171
time, 169–71, 175–76, 181
Tolkien, J. R. R., xix–xxi, 2–5, 13–15, 87,
    115, 139; alchemy, 186–87; on Arwen,
    106; creation myth, 154, 156–57, 171;
    on death, 199–200; end of an age,
    167–68; fairy-stories, 7, 14, 34, 186,
    188; on Galadriel, 110; use of the word
    "god," 126; Green Knight, 186, 191–92;
    invented languages and mythology,
    9, 150; acquainted with C. G. Jung's
    theories, ix, 1; numbers, 189; on Tom
    Bombadil, 80, 104; World War I
    experience, 67–68; on World War II,
    163
torture, 163

totalitarianism, 163, 166, 195
towers, as symbols of knowledge and
    power, 72–76
transcendence, 18–19
transitions, spiritual, 55
tree, as a symbol of the Self, 52
Tree of Life, 197
trickster, archetypal, 77, 82–84
Trinity, 149
trolls, 39, 60, 171–73
trylleeventyr, 34
typology, 14–15

udve, 17
UFO, 174
unconscious, xii–xiii, xvii, 3, 6, 12, 14, 20,
    27, 29–30, 58, 85, 151, 154, 161, 185,
    191; collective, viii, xi, 1–2, 6, 15, 19, 21,
    35, 58, 77, 157, 187, 191, 194
underworld, 63–64, 95

Vikings, 125; shield-maiden, 113
Virgin Mary, 110
Vølve, 171, 177
von Franz, Marie-Louise, 35

war, 66–67
water, as a symbol for the unconscious, 24
weapons, 165
Welles, Orson, 160
Wells, H. G., 160–61
Werfel, Franz, 180
West, L. Jolyon, 166
wind, changing, as a spiritual event, 69–71
wisdom, 134
Wise Old Man, archetype of the spirit,
    xiv, 129
World War I, 2, 67, 87
World War II, vii, 133, 157, 163–64
Wotan, 66

Yama, 184
Ymir, 184

Zarathustra, 169
Zaubermärchen, 34
Zeitgeist, 6